MARCH TO FREEDOM

Impact
Publishing

P.O. Box 55061
Santa Clarita, CA 91385-5061

Please visit the book's website where you may do the following:

- read reviews of *March to Freedom* by Edith Singer
- see pictures of the author speaking in public
- find a study guide with questions for each chapter
- obtain a free review copy for consideration in the classroom
- watch an excerpt of an interview with this Holocaust survivor
  (courtesy of the Simon Wiesenthal Center. Oral History Archive)

www.Impact-Publishing.com

To order books, please contact Adam Kempler
at (661) 373-9383 or Adam@Impact-Publishing.com

MARCH TO
FREEDOM

A MEMOIR OF THE HOLOCAUST

Edith Singer

Impact
Publishing

Santa Clarita, California

For information, contact Impact Publishing:
Email: ImpactPublishing@yahoo.com
Website: www.ImpactPublishing**Online**.com

Library of Congress Control Number: 2008933218
Singer, Edith.
March To Freedom, A Memoir of the Holocaust

ISBN 978-0-9817794-0-9

Cover photograph by Jim Zuckerman
Cover design by Marie Reese

Printed in the United States of America

10 9 8 7 6 5 4 3 2

In memory of my father, Shabtai Slomovits
and my brother Ya'akov (Yanku)

*This book is dedicated to my daughters Ester and Shula,
their children Yael, Yishai, Eve, and Yoni,
and to all my students who asked the questions.*

Contents

Prologue

This book is about how we lived, not how we died.

When I was a little girl and went to Hebrew school and studied the *Bible*, I learned about history and all kinds of miracles like the parting of the Red Sea. As a child, I wondered, how could the miracles be true? I couldn't believe them, but today, if you look at me, I am one of the real miracles: I was condemned to die because I was born Jewish, but I am alive and able to share my experiences.

When I was liberated by the Russian Army on May 8, 1945 in a small German village, I promised myself that I would not talk or think about concentration camps ever again. I knew I would never forget what happened, but I wanted to push those memories out of the new life I would try to build.

Years later, I became a Hebrew school teacher. One day, an eight-year-old student wanted to know what the tattoo on my arm was. "Is that your phone number?" he asked. The question upset me, but I decided, at that moment, that I could no longer hide from or pretend to forget about my past. I felt obligated to educate the new generation about the Holocaust. In the 1960s I started to talk to students from different kinds of schools— Jewish schools, Catholic schools, public schools, and colleges. Every time I prepared to speak to a group, I felt anxious and depressed.

"Again, I must tell my story. Why am I doing this?" I always asked myself. But I had made a promise to go, so I went. When I saw the reactions of the students, I knew I was doing the right thing. I felt I had taught them a very important lesson, and, at the same time, I was showing my father and brother that I had not forgotten them.

As the years passed, fewer and fewer survivors remained. I realized that my stories must live on after me, so I began to write them down. My family inspired and encouraged me.

It was not easy. Every story took me back to Auschwitz and Taucha.[1] After completing each story, I stopped for a few months until I could write again.

One day, I looked over a previously written story and discovered that I had written down details I thought I had forgotten. By writing down my experiences, I let go of some of the painful memories.

I hope that the readers of this book will gain a better understanding of the Holocaust and will unite in the struggle against evil so that it may never happen again.

---

1. A labor camp, not to be confused with Dachau, the death camp.

Before The War

Edith, 1940

Lilly, Frieda, Yanku, Shabtai, and Edith, 1933

Chust, Main Street

1 The Ghetto in Chust

I was born in Chust, Czechoslovakia between the two world wars on August 18, 1927. Chust was a small town of 20,000 gentiles and 5,000 Jews.

My parents raised three children in a religious home. The most important thing in the family was the education of the children. My father worked in the lumber business, and we lived a comfortable, middle-class life in a three-bedroom home. When my parents were born at the beginning of the century, Chust was part of the Austro-Hungarian Empire, so they spoke Hungarian and German, and taught us, too. After World War I, our part of Hungary became Czechoslovakia, so at school we spoke Czech. With my mother, I spoke Hungarian, and with my father, I spoke Yiddish. A large percentage of the European Jews spoke Yiddish, so later when I met Jews in camps from other countries, we could communicate in Yiddish or one of the other languages that I knew.

As far as I can go back in my memory, I always heard adults talking about the War (WWI), and every conversation ended with, "Will there be another?" I also heard the name Hitler before

I could understand the meaning of it. When I was fourteen years old, I dreamed that Hitler came into our little town and into our house and started a fire.

My earliest memories of public school were associated with anti-Semitism; the non-Jewish students and teachers did not hide their prejudice. Even in kindergarten, the teachers forced the Jewish children to sit at separate tables at the back of the room.

One day, I came to school with a bad case of laryngitis. As soon as the music teacher realized that I was hoarse, she called on me to sing a solo. I pleaded with her to excuse me, but she insisted that I stand in front of the class and sing, humiliating me to the point of tears. The entire class laughed and teased me. Another teacher ruined my straight-*A* report card by giving me an undeserved *B* in sewing.

I remember only one teacher, Miss Pearl, an older woman, who was kind to the Jewish children. She stopped her regular lesson to lecture the class about the evils of prejudice. But this did not help because the next day the teasing, the name-calling, and the beatings in the school yard continued. Whenever we were hurt, we went to Miss Pearl, and she comforted us; we loved her for her kindness during this difficult time.

In September 1939, World War II broke out, and Hitler gave our part of Czechoslovakia, known as Carpatorusse, back to Hungary. Overnight, without moving, we found ourselves in Hungary. The language of instruction in my school changed from Czech to Hungarian. This was not a major problem for the children because we learned fast.

With the Hungarian occupation our lives changed completely; the government enacted all types of anti-Semitic laws. Our lives became increasingly difficult. At first, government leaders fired all Jews in public office.

Every few weeks leaders announced new restrictions. We had to bring all our radios, bicycles, sewing machines, and any other machines that had any value to City Hall. City officials distributed all these items among the non-Jewish population of Chust.

The biggest blow came when one day they said, "Any Jew who has any kind of business, bring the keys to City Hall." City officials took the keys, and non-Jews lined up from our home town—people with whom I, my parents, and probably my grandparents grew up for generations—to take the keys. They had already picked out which stores they wanted. These people moved into these private businesses full of merchandise without paying a penny.

Perhaps because we lived two houses back from the street, in an alley, we managed to hide our radio. At night, some of our Jewish neighbors used to come over, and we closed all the doors, windows, and curtains, and tried to listen to the London broadcast. We were hoping that the Hungarian news was not true. If the news was good, we believed it. If it was bad, we told ourselves it must be German propaganda.

The Hungarians expelled to Poland some Jews who did not have Hungarian citizenship papers. A few managed to sneak back to our town and told us what was happening there: the Nazis forced Jews to dig their own mass graves and then shot them. The Nazis set up camps surrounded by electrified wires. I did not believe this was true and would not accept that this could happen to our family. I always ran to another room because I didn't want to hear those stories. I thought, if I don't hear them, I won't know them. It cannot happen to me. But the news worried and scared my parents.

Administrators allowed my class to complete junior high school; however, they would not allow all the other Jewish students who were one class level below me to attend public school anymore. The Czechs built a very large high school called Gymnasium. All the children from the surrounding villages used to come and study there. Even though we knew that they wouldn't accept me, my mother took me to the principal and showed him my report card when I finished junior high school. He stared at the report card and then looked at me. He told Mother, "I would love to have her in my school, but I cannot take her because she is Jewish." Parents set up private schools in their homes so that their children could continue their studies; this was happening until 1944.

Outside of school, life was hard too. We never knew what would happen next. The anti-Semites preyed upon every Jewish man, woman, and child.

The Hungarian army drafted Jewish young men at 21, but not in the regular way. The army took them away in the middle of the night, during weddings, etc. The young men did not report for duty; the army came and got them. Also, the Hungarian army did not draft them to the regular army: they drafted the Jewish men to labor camps. The Jews had to wear their own clothing and a yellow arm band. Once the army took them away, they were not allowed to write home. We didn't know where they were, what they were doing, or who was alive. We had no communication with them. We had to wait until the war ended to see who survived.

One day, my father came home with his beard shaved off. For the first time in my life, I saw my father without his beard, which he wore for religious reasons. When we asked him what happened, he told us that a Hungarian soldier grabbed him on the street, took him to a barber shop, and ordered the barber, "Shave the beard off this Jew!"

Often, on a train or bus, a non-Jew would demand that a Jew give up his or her seat or move to the last compartment. Many times a drunk who needed money would grab a Jew on the street, take him to the police station, and lie to an officer saying, "This Jew took my money!" The police officer would order the Jew to give the drunkard all the money he had. The innocent man was then beaten and thrown into jail for a few days without even being questioned.

All these experiences made our lives difficult, but we were

still together in our homes, and we were not hungry. These hardships went on until March 21, 1944. I was sixteen years old.

By 1944, the world knew that the Germans were losing the war. It was only a question of time, and we were hoping and praying that we would be able to stay home until the war ended.

One morning, we woke up and realized that the German army had occupied all of Hungary. At that point, our lives changed rapidly from bad to tragic.

On the second day of occupation, the Germans arrested all the Jewish leaders—doctors, lawyers, and rabbis. Some non-Jews who knew the Jewish population of Chust collaborated with the Nazis to prepare this list of leaders. The government ordered us to sew yellow stars to the clothing on our chests, and they enforced a curfew from dusk to dawn on the Jewish population. Officials rationed food only for the Jews and forbade Kosher meat. These orders came so fast that we had no time to grasp what was happening; we had no leaders to whom we could turn.

Whatever the Germans did in other occupied countries over the course of several years, they accomplished in Hungary in just a few weeks. Hitler placed Adolph Eichmann in charge of the Hungarian Jews, and Eichmann wanted to liquidate the Jews quickly because he knew the war would not last forever. After only one month of the German occupation, they told us to take whatever we could fit on a horse-drawn wagon and go to the ghetto. We put mattresses, clothing, food, dishes, pictures, books, valuables—whatever we thought was most important—on the wagon. We struggled to assemble one cartload from a lifetime of belongings. My father did not even lock the door behind us. He knew that our non-Jewish neighbors would loot everything.

The ghetto in Chust consisted of a few blocks of homes, about a square mile, enclosed by a high, barbed-wire fence. Five thousand Jews were forced to live in this small area.

The Nazis assigned my family to a house that belonged to one of our cousins, an average, three-bedroom house; more than fifty people lived in this house. My parents, Frieda and Shabtai, both forty-three; my twenty-year-old sister, Lilly; my eighteen-year-old brother, Yanku, and I were in one small room with two additional families—fourteen people in all. Every family had its own corner for their belongings.

We brought our mattresses from home and spread them out on the floor at night. All three families slept one next to the other. During the day, we piled the mattresses up in a corner so that we could move around in the room and get to our suitcases. When we wanted to change clothes, we held up a make-shift curtain for privacy. But, our family was still together, and we were not yet hungry.

We brought all of our food from home, which lasted for the four weeks we were in the ghetto. We did not have to depend on the meager rations the Germans provided. The Mothers alternated cooking and even competed with each other over who could make a better meal. We ate together, and after the meals the girls washed the dishes. It didn't occur to us that boys could wash dishes too (but now my husband washes a lot of dishes).

Often, the adults fought with each other over trivial things. Everyone's nerves were on edge.

When the Germans were not around, the adults gathered the children in one of the rooms and taught them whatever they could: a doctor taught biology, an engineer taught math, a rabbi taught Hebrew. They wanted their children to go on with their schooling.

The older boys tried to learn some self-defense tactics to protect themselves against confrontations with the Nazis. My brother Yanku, among others, led this group. Whatever he knew or read about in books, he taught to the younger boys. They did not know that they would never have a chance to protect themselves against what the Germans had planned for them.

Every morning, officers from the Gestapo[1] came to the ghetto. When they arrived, everybody immediately busied him- or herself; we grabbed a broom and swept our rooms or the yard

---

1. The German secret state police.

outside. We had to show them that we worked.

Each time the Gestapo came, all the men had to line up. We feared the Gestapo because we never knew what they wanted. Usually, they picked a group of young men and took them to work somewhere outside the city, bringing them back late in the evening.

One day, the Gestapo picked Yanku to go to work. My father did not talk the whole day; he paced back and forth from our cramped room to the gate of the ghetto. It became dark, and Yanku was not back yet. That day the first rumors of taking us "away" surfaced, fueling my father's panic. Finally, the group of young men returned to the ghetto. My father saw Yanku, ran to him, and burst out crying. I had never seen my father cry before this. Later, he told my mother that he was afraid Yanku would not return in time to be with us when we were taken away from the ghetto.

In the beginning of May 1944, four weeks after we had arrived in the ghetto, the Gestapo told us, "Get ready. In two days, we will relocate you for work." When they said "relocate you for work," they included older people, disabled people, little children, babies, pregnant women, everybody. They told us that we could take with us only what we could carry in our hands and on our backs and march to the train station, so we had to decide again what to pick, from the few belongings that we brought from home, to take with us in suitcases and knapsacks. Of course, the young Mothers with children couldn't carry anything because they carried their babies, or their children held on to their skirts. We tried to figure out what to take. We put on two sweaters, or two sets of socks, or two sets of underwear to have more. I also put on my best blue shoes.

We tried to hide jewelry and money. We didn't know where we were going. I overheard my father saying to my mother, "Put away this ring. Maybe we will be able to buy bread with it." I looked at my father, and I couldn't understand what a ring had to do with bread, but later I learned what he meant.

We walked to the train station. The people carried as much as they could hold in their two hands; the children held on tightly to their dolls and Teddy bears. Five thousand people, young and old, carrying all kinds of suitcases, knapsacks made from sheets, baskets, and wrapped bundles, marched in silence.

Our frightened group walked three miles to the train station. People abandoned the streets. The non-Jewish population of Chust hid inside their houses. Our neighbors—people we had worked with, grown up with, gone to school with, and played with—became invisible. They did not come out to say goodbye, to give us something for our journey, or to promise to take care of our homes until we returned. Nothing. Empty streets. Only a large, silent group of Jews walked to the station accompanied by the Hungarian police and Gestapo.

When we arrived at the train station, we saw girls sitting behind long tables. I looked at the girls; almost all of them were my former classmates from junior high school. All of us had to register by giving our names before we left. None of the girls looked at me, showed recognition, or gave me reassurance. They just sat, joking, smiling, laughing, and taking our names. I looked at them, and I became very sad, but I didn't say anything. After the registration, the officials searched every man, woman, and child in tents; they searched our clothes, our luggage, and our bodies for hidden money and jewelry. When they found something, not only did they take it away, but they beat up the person very badly. If we could easily reach the hidden jewelry and money, we threw it away to avoid a beating. Jewelry and money covered the ground.

They searched Yanku, and they found money that my mother had sewn into his jacket lapel. A Hungarian policeman began to hit him.

"Please, don't hurt my son," my father pleaded. "I have more money. I'll give you everything. Just don't hit him." My father undid his hernia belt, opened up a seam, and gave the policeman all he had.

Then, they pushed us into cattle trains that took us away from Chust to the unknown.

2 Arrival in Auschwitz

The locomotive pulled a long row of cattle cars behind it. The cargo—Jews. I was in one of the cattle cars with my family, along with eighty other people from my hometown, Chust.

It was extremely crowded and stuffy inside. The only fresh air came from two tiny windows with bars at the top of the cattle car. Wooden planks lined the floor. The soldiers gave us a few buckets—some were filled with water, and the others were for toilet use. When we had to use the toilet, someone would hold a blanket up for privacy.

We brought food with us for the journey, but no one could eat. I remember a bag of butter cookies my mother had baked "for the road." Later, in concentration camp, during the longest year of my life, I often thought about those cookies; I could not forgive myself for not eating more of them when I could.

For the first two days, the Hungarian police guarded the trains. Then the Gestapo and the SS[1] took over. They rode on top

1. The elite military units of the Nazi Party who used terror and destruction to achieve their goals.

of the train with their machine guns aimed at us. The journey lasted for several days, and we had no idea where we were going. After the third day, I felt so exhausted and tired that I only had one thing on my mind: when will I arrive wherever I am going so that I can wash up and go to sleep in a bed?

The soldiers opened the cattle cars once a day to empty the buckets and to provide fresh water. Every time the guards opened the doors, they took two or three men as hostages from each car. The guards demanded money and jewelry for the hostages' return. We heard shots but could not see what was happening. Even though the soldiers had searched us thoroughly before entering the trains, some people managed to hide a few valuables. Those who had hidden money or jewelry gave it up to save the hostages. The hostages from my cattle car always returned.

After four days of traveling, the train stopped again, but this time the soldiers did not open the doors for water or bucket changes. We waited for one hour, two, three, and then we stopped counting.

We could not bear the hot, stale air, the stench, the crying of children, the moaning of the sick, and the uncertainty. Night fell, and we were still inside the train. We remained locked inside without fresh water for over twenty-four hours. We did not know where we were or what awaited us. We heard talking outside but could not reach the two little windows to look out and see what was going on.

Finally, the doors of the cattle cars opened. We all rushed forward to get some fresh air and see what was going on outside. I was in the first row; my father stood next to me, and my mother stood next to him. We saw barbed wire everywhere. We saw German SS soldiers and officers with their machine guns and snarling German Shepherds. We also saw men in gray and blue striped clothing who were much shorter than the soldiers.

I saw a large sign in a half circle with the word "Auschwitz" on it. I did not know what it meant, and I had never seen this name. We had heard of other concentration camps: Treblinka,

Theresienstadt, Dachau, but not Auschwitz.[2] Under "Auschwitz" were the words "Arbeit Macht Frei" (Work Makes You Free). It made no sense to me.

My father stood in the open door looking around silently and said to us, "I see people in striped uniforms, like in a prison. It means they don't kill everybody. We will obey all the rules, and we will survive." I looked at my father's sad face—I was sixteen—and only then did I begin to understand his fears and the seriousness of the situation.

"Raus, schnell!" (Out, quickly!) the Germans shouted at us. We had to jump out of the trains onto the ground, three feet below. It was most difficult for the elderly and the sick. No ladders or platforms were set up, but we helped each other as much as we could.

We all had some kind of baggage with us—a knapsack, a suitcase, a small parcel. As we jumped down, we heard the next order, "Put your belongings there!" I looked "there" and saw a mountain of baggage—all shapes, sizes, and colors.

How will I find my bags if they are all thrown over there? I thought. I didn't put my name on them. I did not know they would never be returned to me.

We formed a wall of silent people.

"Schnell, schnell, schnell! Men here, women there!" they shouted from a loud speaker. This divided every family. Everything happened so quickly and unexpectedly that we did not even have a chance to think. Then, everyone tried to talk to each other at the same time; we could not understand much.

Standing in line with all the women and children, I looked over at the men's side. I wanted another glance, another word from my father and brother. Suddenly, my tall father looked so small. His confident, warm smile that always comforted me as a child was gone. For a moment our eyes met. My father shouted in Yiddish, "Nekomeh! Nekomeh!" (Revenge! Revenge!) I was

---

2. Auschwitz may have been the best kept secret in Europe. It was the largest camp, killing the most people—between 1.1-1.6 million people.

too far away. All I could do was wave.

The men in striped clothing herded us towards the main gate. They processed the new transports.[3] Whenever they got close to us, they whispered in Yiddish, "Gibt die kleine kinder zu die alte mentschen" (Give the small children to the old people or relatives). I understood the words, but I did not know what they meant.

These men were the "old-timers" of Auschwitz, prisoners who knew what was going on, and they tried to warn us.

The Mothers panicked and clutched their children closer to themselves. The line kept moving.

"Gibt die kleine kinder zu die alte mentschen!" the prisoners insisted. "You will have to work, but the old folks can take care of the children. Give them, quickly, before it's too late."

They could not tell the Mothers the truth. The old-timers knew that women with young children were to be killed right away. Hesitantly, some Mothers handed their children over to their older relatives believing they would be safe, fed, and taken care of. By separating the Mothers from their children, the old-timers managed to save a few young women.

Later, we heard that at the beginning of the war soldiers used to take away babies from healthy-looking Mothers, but after they grabbed the babies by force, the Mothers would scream and protest hysterically. The Nazis disliked this, so by the time the Hungarian Jews arrived at the end of the war, the soldiers just sent the Mothers with the children to the gas chambers without any resistance.

My favorite aunt, Judith, had eight children. The three oldest boys went with their father. She held her baby in her arms; her four other children clung tightly to her skirt. She would not leave them. "I cannot, I cannot!" she cried. The soldiers sent all of them to the gas chambers.

Very few people gave up their children. I later met a woman

---

3. Nazi term for trainloads of people arriving in Auschwitz.

in Los Angeles who had five little boys with her when she was sent to Auschwitz. She gave the boys up; the Nazis killed them. She survived the war and later remarried but never had more children.

We moved closer and closer to the main gate. I held on to my mother and sister. Because I was short, I stood on my tip-toes to see what was going on. We saw a group of German SS officers, soldiers, and old-timers (women in striped clothing). A high-ranking SS officer faced us. Tall, with dark hair, wearing white gloves and an impeccable SS uniform, he talked little. We saw from his uniform and demeanor that he was in charge of everything. The other officers knew exactly what every move-ment meant. He held a small pointer in his hand and smiled at us. He was the most handsome man I had ever seen—he was Dr. Mengele, "the Angel of Death."

With a slight movement of his pointer, he directed us to the right or to the left. This little movement of his gloved hand determined our fate: right meant life; left meant death. Who went to the right? All young women and a few adoles-cent girls who were physically developed and looked older and women who were 45-50 and who looked younger. This group had a chance for life—not all survived—but they had a chance. All the others—the older people, the young Mothers with children or babies, the disabled, and the pregnant women who "showed"—went to the left. The Nazis gassed and cre-mated them the same day. Nobody ever saw any of those people alive again.

Mengele looked at my aunt, Hankaneni, who stood next to us and asked her, "Wie alt bist du?" (How old are you?)

"Funf und dreisig," (Thirty-five) she answered quickly. She was close to fifty. Mengele let her go with her two teenage daughters. Her fast thinking saved her life.

Dr. Mengele sent my mother, sister, and me to the right with-out questions. This was the first time, but not the last, that we would meet Dr. Mengele.

On our way to the Entlausung (delousing) building, we

passed a small podium where several prisoners played classical music.[4] I did not know why. We continued marching and saw strange-looking people with shaved heads behind barbed wires, women who were screaming and motioning wildly to us, "Give us your food! Throw us whatever you have. You won't be able to hold on to anything. Please, give us some bread!" We did not understand, and we did not believe them. I thought they were the insane inmates of the camp. Later, we understood; they were not crazy. They used to be like us, and we were becoming like them.

We arrived at a huge concrete building. In the first room the guards told us to undress and stand in line. I felt shocked, embarrassed, and frightened; I tried in vain to cover myself with my arms. Later, we found out that this was an everyday scene for the SS soldiers and male prisoners who shuffled us from room to room. They told us to leave all of our clothing behind, except for our shoes. I clutched my blue shoes. If we had any hidden money or jewelry still, it was gone now because we were undressed completely.

A line of female old-timers holding hair clippers shaved our heads and the hair from the rest of our bodies. We really did not have anything anymore. They pushed us to the next room. We put our shoes by the wall and went back into the center of the room. Suddenly, cold water sprayed us from the ceiling. We had no soap or towels. The shower lasted a few minutes. In the next room another group of old-timers sprayed us with disinfectant powder, the kind one uses to spray animals against fleas and lice. At the last stop, before going outside again, we received clothing: one pair of underwear and one dress. In 1944, the Nazis did not have striped clothing to distribute anymore. With this strange clothing and shaved heads, we hardly recognized one another. My mother, sister, and I held each other tightly, so as not to get separated in the mass of anonymous bodies.

We were outside when the SS guards ordered us to stand

4. The Nazis used music to distract new arrivals and allay their suspicions. It was also for their own enjoyment.

Appell (roll call) for the first time. We had to line up quickly, five people to a row. The guards counted us, and then took 1,000 women to Camp C, which held about 30,000 women, and to Barrack 26.

We were exhausted and hungry. Maybe now we will receive some warm food and go to bed, I thought. But in Camp C, we stood Appell for several more hours.

Our Blockaelteste,[5] Eitu—a Jewish girl, an old-timer—told us about Auschwitz. We did not believe the horrors she told us. "You were still in your homes with your families when I was already here. You had enough food when I was hungry," she screamed at us.

Finally, they gave us our first meal—a piece of black, mud-like bread, a tiny square of margarine, and one thin slice of salami. We could not eat the bread and left it on the ground. The old-timers immediately snatched it up. Very quickly we learned that there was no choice of food, and we ate whatever we were given.

We entered a huge, empty barrack with no beds. One thousand women slept on the bare concrete floor. We had to lie on top of each other; sleep was impossible. Just as we dozed off, someone started to scream. Then another woman screamed, then another, and soon the hysterical screaming of a thousand women filled the barrack. I held my mother's and sister's hands. "We are not going to scream," I told them. The Blockaelteste came out from her private corner and shouted at us to quiet down.

At 3:00 a.m. the Blockaelteste roused us by yelling again, this time to get up and out. It was pitch black and very cold when our first day in Auschwitz began.

---

5. Chief of the barrack, often a prisoner trusted by the SS, who had disciplinary powers over other inmates.

3 *Appell*

The Nazis ordered us to stand Appell when it was still dark. They counted us twice a day—once, early in the morning and again in the late afternoon—before we received our daily ration of food.

The Germans designed an open area between the rows of barracks specifically for Appell. In this area, the gravel ground rose a little bit in the middle. We formed lines—five people to a row, two columns of five hundred women from each barrack.

During the morning Appell, it was extremely cold. We stood very close to each other, using our body heat for warmth. Some people pushed and yelled because everyone tried to be in the middle of the five-person row to get the maximum warmth from bodies on both sides. My mother always said to the people in our line, "I will stand at the end of our line as long as you let my two daughters stay in the middle." She was so small and fragile, yet she always wanted to shelter us from the cold.

Later, after the Nazis separated me from my mother and sister, I decided to stand at the end of the line so that I could toughen myself for the future. If, one day, I would not be in the middle of the line, I wanted to be strong enough to survive the cold on the outside of the line. But after one try on the outside, I felt so cold and miserable that I fought my way back to the middle. I decided that I would harden myself for the cold when I had no other choice.

We stood Appell for several hours, our shivering bodies huddled together. We never knew what time it was. Slowly, the darkness faded, and the sun came out.

"The SS are coming! Straighten up!" The warning spread quickly through the rows. A group of thirty SS officers marched into our camp—one officer for each barrack. They had a very efficient system for counting us: they took one look and could see immediately if there were five people to a row. The counting itself went very fast: five-ten-fifteen-twenty. If the prisoners' attendance matched their roll call numbers, the Appell was over. However, if even one prisoner was missing—if someone was too sick to come out, if someone was asleep in a dark corner of the barrack, or if someone had died during the night—then all 30,000 prisoners had to stand or kneel for hours until the officers found the missing prisoner.

At first, the kneeling caused only a humiliating discomfort, but as the hours passed it evolved into physical torture. The gravel cut into our knees. We tucked our dresses under our knees, but this only made it worse because later we had to tear the dress off of our bloodied skin. Our bodies ached, but if someone tried to move or shift position, an SS guard or Kapo[1] would be there immediately with his whip on our backs.

The next day our knees swelled up from gravel cuts and infections. There was nothing we could do.

The afternoon Appell started a few hours after lunch. We had barely settled into our bare, wooden bunk beds when they ordered us to go outside again.

The high sun burned our shaved heads. We missed the hair

1. A prisoner put in charge of other prisoners.

that would have protected us from cold and heat. Some women
who were lucky received a very big dress, and they tore a piece
off of the bottom and wore it on their heads. Our lips burned and
cracked too. No matter when I came to line up, all the places in
the shade along the barracks were taken. The SS finally came to
count us at about five o'clock in the afternoon. We couldn't bear
standing in line for so many hours. The weak and sick women
sank to the ground and sat on the gravel.

One SS officer came by every day just before the actual
counting. The warning spread, "He is coming!" Quickly, we
helped up those who were sitting, and we all straightened up.
He walked by our lines slowly, with a big stick in his hand and a
mocking smile on his face. He picked several women out from
our lines and beat them severely.

"Why did you sit down! You know you have to stand and wait
until you are counted!" he screamed at them.

If some of us tried to defend the woman saying she did not sit
down, the beatings became worse. We could not understand how
he always picked the right women—the ones who had actually
sat down—since everyone was standing by the time he got to
our lines. Finally, we figured out that he looked at the backs of
our dresses, and if he saw dirt on them, he knew who had sat on
the ground. From that point on we always made sure to brush off
our dresses.

One morning, a month after our arrival, a group of Kapos
appeared at the end of Appell. They handed us blank post-
cards and pencils and ordered us to "write home." It seemed
very strange.

"You will write that you are doing fine. You are working and
receiving good food. Your families are together, and everyone is
taken care of."

I wrote what I was told, but when I turned the postcard over
to address it, I realized there was no one to send it to. Not one
person in my home town cared about my well being, so I turned
it in unaddressed.

One evening after Appell, the officers told us to undress and line up again inside the barrack. As we moved down the line, they sprayed us with disinfectant. Then, unexpectedly, they gave us a clean set of clothing: one dress and one pair of underwear. Luck determined what size we received. Lilly and I got dresses in our size, but my mother received a very small one that didn't even cover her body. We told her to sneak into the line again and try to get another dress. She did, but Eitu caught her and slapped her across the face brutally; blood gushed from her cracked lips.

"Why did you hit our mother?" Lilly screamed at Eitu.

"Look what you did! Her lips are bleeding!" I yelled.

Eitu became enraged and was just about to hit us too when her sister came to our rescue. She took us aside and washed the blood off my mother's face with a clean rag. Without a word, Eitu gave my mother a larger dress.

Every day after Appell, Mother, Lilly, and I felt grateful that we returned to our barrack together. We tried not to think of the days ahead and what might happen to us; I prayed for the day when I would not have to stand in line for Appell.

Ever since then, I have had an aversion for standing in lines, especially for anything that is not essential, such as movies, amusement parks, and restaurants.

4 Lunch

Morning Appell ended, but the SS did not allow us to return to the barracks until a few appointed prisoners had cleaned them. But what was there to clean? The wooden bunks were bare, and no one had any food or belongings. They forced us to wait for hours as some prisoners raked the dirt floors and emptied the toilet buckets.

Some people tried to push their way to the cold water faucets to wash up a little or drink from their cupped palms.

At mid-morning the SS allowed us to return to the barracks. We went to the bunk beds where we could lie on one side, or we sat with our legs tucked under our chins and did nothing. We could not talk to each other because the Blockaelteste demanded silence.

It seemed like an eternity until they told us to go outside again. Lunch time was approaching; thirty thousand women lined up in several rows to receive their meager bowls of soup. In this soup, the Germans put bromide, a tranquilizer.

When we first arrived, Auschwitz terrified us. Someone would cry out, "Look, there is gas! They are poisoning us." We all screamed and cried in terror. Mass hysteria could break out at any time.

Two or three weeks after our arrival, the screaming stopped, and all the women stopped menstruating: the old-timers told us that the bromide did this.

The old-timers who worked in the kitchen brought out large kettles of soup. A few women who had somehow obtained a small bowl risked a beating by running to the open kettle to scoop up some soup, a difficult and dangerous undertaking, but hunger overtook all reasoning. The rest of us—thousands of hungry women—waited in line as they passed out military canteens and spoons, which they collected after lunch.

As we moved along the line, the excitement grew. Which part of the soup will I get? Will it be from the top of the kettle and very watery? Or will it be from the bottom of the kettle, a bit thicker, with some small pieces of vegetables in it? But no matter what part of the soup we got, it always tasted horrible. No one washed the vegetables, and we felt the grit of sand between our teeth. It took us a few days to learn to eat this soup. My mother forced herself to eat her soup and some of ours. She told us that she liked it so that in the evening she could give us half of her bread, saying she had eaten enough at lunch.

Some prisoners snuck into other lines to try to get a second helping. If the SS who watched us during lunch time caught them, they beat them. The guards walked among the prisoners with their whips ready. They enjoyed seeing how far a hungry person would go for a little extra watery soup.

Occasionally, the SS guards would let a few prisoners go for a second bowl of soup, and just as they started to eat, the guards would jump on the surprised victims and beat them. Sometimes the guards let the prisoners finish the second helping and then attacked them.

In the beginning, we did not understand how the guards knew who had eaten twice. In time, we realized that when the SS saw two canteens next to one prisoner or when someone came to take soup and her dish was not clean, she was getting a second bowl of soup. We had to learn all these tricks to avoid being caught and punished; it was part of the struggle for survival.

After lunch, we still felt hungry. Again, they left us outside. We had nothing to do but feel our hunger and misery and wait for the next order.

The hardest thing to endure in Auschwitz was the constant, unsubsiding hunger. We felt so hungry all the time that we thought about that the most. We felt cold and miserable too, but hungry all the time. No words in any language could describe this hunger.

Wandering around the camp, we met some relatives, friends, or neighbors from other barracks. We talked and sought comfort from each other. Once, I overheard some older women talking.

"Do you realize where we are? We will never get out of here alive!"

"Yes, I know where we are," the other women answered. "Through the gate we came in and through the chimney we will go out."

That scared me. I knew I could not go on if I were so terrified all the time. I wanted to survive. I had to find a way of going on, a way to resist the Germans and stay alive.

I will not listen to people who are pessimistic and who do not believe in a future, I thought to myself. If God wants me to die, then it can happen anytime, anywhere, even after the war, even on my way home. But if God wants me to live, no German or anyone else can harm me.

The day passed slowly. We still felt hungry, and the guards left us standing outside. By this time, the sun burned high in the sky. We looked for a shady place to stand, but other prisoners occupied the few places next to the walls of the barracks.

Then the shouting began again. "Everybody inside. Quickly! Move!" We ran into the barracks and crawled onto the bunk beds. Lunch at Auschwitz ended.

5 Sleeping

We were sleeping fitfully on our wooden bunk beds when the lights in the barrack went on and Eitu the Blockaelteste and her Kapos shouted at us.

"Aufstein, raus, schnell!" (Get up! Everybody outside! Fast!) We had to jump down from our bunk beds and run outside.

The bunk beds were three levels high—bare wooden planks with no mattresses, no blankets, and no pillows. Fifteen women slept on each level like herrings—seven in one direction, seven in the opposite direction, and one person who wasn't fast enough had to lie across the middle on top of everyone's legs. We only had room to lie on one side; our bones hurt from lying on the wood. If one person wanted to turn to the other side, all fifteen women had to turn also. Lying on one side for hours, without moving, was unbearable. Our bones ached, our legs cramped, and numbness spread through our bodies. Because of lack of room, the women kicked each other a lot.

"Please, let's turn to the other side," my sister Lilly said one night.

"No, not yet!" answered the woman next to her. "I am still all right, and my sister is asleep already."

Lilly waited in pain and then begged again, "Let's turn now, please!" No one moved; Lilly could not wait any longer and started to kick her neighbors until everyone turned to the other side.

Almost every night an upper bunk collapsed, sending the startled women crashing down to the second level and then to the bottom level. They got hurt and started to scream. Eitu rushed in, shouting at everyone to be quiet, and ordered the bunk bed fixed. Two of her helpers brought in a hammer and nails and repaired the bunk bed.

In spite of the terrible sleeping conditions, we could only escape the reality of Auschwitz through sleep. When we slept, we felt no hunger, pain, or misery.

Sometimes, when Eitu left the barrack, we talked quietly to each other; we talked about our families, our homes, and our lives before Auschwitz. We only used each other's first names because last names were not important, and we tried to make friends, to be in a group, and to sleep in the same bunk bed.

One young woman, Klari, told us that she had married her high school sweetheart, but the Nazis took him to a forced labor camp right after the wedding ceremony. She never saw him again.

"Do you mean to say that you are a married woman and still a virgin?" we teased her. For a few moments, we laughed together, and from that day on we called Klari the "Virgin Wife."

She made us think about our own romantic futures. Would we live to meet a young man, to know what love is, to get married and have children?

Friendly and optimistic, a Jewish Hungarian woman in her early forties read palms, always predicting a bright future for everyone who came to her. I watched her reading the palms of other women, and then I too stretched out my hand. She looked at it closely.

"Oh, darling, you have a very long life line," she said.

"What does that mean?" I asked.

"You will live a long time, eighty or ninety years."

"You mean I will survive this hell? I'll go home to my family? I'll eat a lot of bread?" I asked excitedly.

"Of course, darling," she reassured me. "You will find your family, and one day you will have your own children, and you will be happy again."

I thanked her and walked away, determined to believe what she told me.

Luckily, sometimes we dreamed pleasant dreams. One night, I dreamed that I was home with my family for the Sabbath dinner; the candles flickered in the silver candlesticks. The large challah[1] lay under the embroidered cover. Dressed in our best Sabbath clothes, we stood around the table and listened to my father bless the wine and bread. Just as I reached out to get my thick slice of challah, I felt an elbow jabbing me in the stomach.

"What's going on? Why are you hitting me?" I asked the girl lying next to me.

"You stretched out your hand and almost poked my eye out!" she answered angrily.

I tried to go back to sleep and enter my dream world of home again, but instead I heard the screaming of the Blockaelteste, "Aufstehen, aufstehen!"

Quickly, we put on our shoes which we used as pillows. We slept in our only dress. The shouting became louder and louder. We wanted so badly to hold onto our precious moments of sleep, but the Blockaelteste ordered us to run outside where we joined the thousands of women from the other barracks.

Eitu stood in the open doorway with a large club in her hand, pushing, shouting, and hitting us as we ran out. One thousand women could not possibly get out of the barrack at once. Everyone tried to be in the middle of the pushing crowd to avoid the painful blows of Eitu's stick.

No SS guards stood around at this time. Eitu did not have to

---

1. The traditional loaf of rich white bread, usually braided or twisted, eaten by Jews on the Sabbath and holidays.

impress them with her cruelty, yet she hit us anyway.

It was dark and cold outside, and the lights on top of the electrified fences reminded the prisoners that the slightest touch of the wires meant instant electrocution. In this eerie light, thousands of women moved toward the latrine.

6 Latrine

One barrack at the end of our camp was the latrine. Inside, three long, raised concrete rows with hundreds of holes cut into them served as our toilets. We could use them from either side. Thirty thousand women had to use this latrine within a very short period of time.

It was dark inside. I held my mother's and sister's hands so as not to lose them. Pushing and screaming, people tried to find an unoccupied hole. The Nazis provided no toilet paper; the prisoners often soiled the concrete with excrement. However, a few cold water faucets lined the wall. We had to push our way there to find some water to wash up.

One day, after the morning Appell, Eitu looked for prisoners to do some work. Without knowing the nature of the work, I volunteered.

Eitu took twenty girls from our barrack to the latrine where two Kapos waited for us. They gave us large shovels and several wheel barrows and told us to clean the latrine; we looked at each other in shock. I almost vomited from the stench, but I knew there was no turning back. I took a shovel and started to work.

I don't care what kind of work it is, I thought to myself as I shoveled excrement. It was better to work than to languish in the barracks dreaming of food, waiting for the next order, and wasting away.

When we finished the cleaning, the Kapos told me to stand at the doorway and not let anyone in. Many prisoners came by and wanted to use the latrine, but I had to say, "No."

A woman clutching her stomach and doubled over in pain came running to the door. "May I go inside?" she asked me anxiously.

"No, you cannot," I answered.

"But I have to. I'm sick," she pleaded.

"You know that no one is allowed to go in at this time," I told her.

She did not leave; she looked at me with sad eyes. "Please let me in. Please!" she begged.

Her voice sounded familiar; I looked at her closely. Even with her shaven head and her body shrunken from starvation, I recognized her. She had been my high school science teacher just a few months ago, before we were taken to Auschwitz. She had been a good-looking, friendly woman, and her students had loved her. She stood before me in a badly fitting, dirty dress. Her torn shoes showed that she wore no socks.

"Margitneni?" I asked in a friendlier tone.

She looked at me in amazement. She did not recognize me, and she did not ask how I knew her. "Yes, I am Margitneni. Will you let me in?"

I looked around. With no one watching, I opened the door.

"Quick!" I whispered, and she ran into the latrine.

Inside our barrack at the far end, the guards set up eight buckets for toilet use. They served the one thousand women prisoners when they were not allowed to go outside to the latrine. At other times, the guards used the same buckets for drinking water.

We asked Eitu to let us use the buckets. "If you behave and stay very quiet, I will let you go later," she told us.

We tried to stay quiet, but some of the women cried out in pain, "Please, let me go! I cannot wait any longer. I am sick."

"Quiet!" Eitu shouted. "I told you to behave." Finally, after endless waiting, she announced, "Line up, don't push, and don't talk."

Some of the women jumped down from their bunk beds. The strong ones had to help the weak and sick ones down.

We always stood in a long line for the buckets. Many women who had dysentery could not wait for their turn and soiled themselves and the area around them. This always brought a beating from Eitu or her helpers.

One morning, my sister and I stood in line waiting to use the buckets. Because we stood at the end of the line, we had to wait for a long time. I felt as if I were going to explode, but I was too scared to let go. An excruciating pain racked my body, and I burst out crying.

"Hold on," Lilly told me, knowing what would happen if I did not. She held my hand and reassured me over and over, "We are almost there."

Somehow, I made it to the buckets and avoided a beating.

7 Organizieren

At first, I thought it was just a bad nightmare; I would soon wake up and find myself at home in my own bed, covered with a big feather comforter, my family around me, and plenty of food in the kitchen. But after several days in Auschwitz, I realized that this was not a bad dream but a terrible and cruel reality. My previous life in the little town of Chust now became just images that lived in my memory. Sometimes I wondered if it ever existed—it seemed so far away, so unreachable. The constant hunger, the endless waiting from one order to the next, the milling around with nothing to do—that became my new reality.

I felt very hungry in Auschwitz—so hungry that food dominated my thoughts. We received two meager meals a day: for lunch, a bowl of watery vegetable soup, and for dinner, a small piece of dark, coarse bread, one thin slice of salami, and a square of margarine. This food—between 450 and 500 calories—nourished us for 24 hours. We felt hungry all the time.

The bread looked and tasted like mud. The first few days, we couldn't eat it. We dropped it on the floor; the old timers grabbed it. As soon as we realized that we had no choice, then we started to eat the bread, and we prayed for more. We heard that they added sawdust to the flour because in 1944 they didn't have much food left in Germany, and it tasted like sawdust. They divided this little loaf of bread, maybe a pound, in five pieces. Every row of five people received one loaf, one slice per person. When the bread came, everybody started shaking. We thought, will I get an end piece or a middle piece? Will it be a bigger piece or a smaller piece? Every bite counted. The girls who worked in the kitchen and cut the bread didn't measure the slices, so luck determined what we received. We never received enough. We ate the bread fast the minute we received it, and then we had to wait until the next day to eat. The hunger did not subside. The bread was just a taste; it didn't satisfy us at all.

I always fantasized about having enough bread to feel full. I had a little prayer: if I am to die here, I would rather die today than tomorrow so that I will be hungry one day less. My other prayer was: if I have to die, just once more I would like to have enough food to remember what it is like not to be hungry. I had another wish too. If I could live through the war and be liberated, I wanted two dresses, so that I could wear one and wash the other.

When I saw the guards taking people away to be killed, I always felt so bad for them because they were suffering for so many weeks or months, and then the guards killed them anyway.

I, like many other prisoners, always looked for some extra food. When new prisoners arrived and marched through the main gate, we asked them to throw us whatever food they still had with them. We knew that the guards would take away all their possessions, but they did not know this, and most of them held on to their belongings.

We had various means of obtaining extra food, shoes, a scarf, a needle and thread, and other necessities. This was called "organizieren"—to organize something for oneself. Organizieren involved standing around the kitchen when a truck delivered carrots and turnips and snatching the fallen ones. Organizieren meant receiving a little extra soup for helping the girl who served lunch. Organizieren involved grabbing a piece of clothing from an open storage building. As long as we obtained the object without stealing from another prisoner, we called it organizieren.

Electrified barbed wire fences ran between the camps in Auschwitz. We often stood by the fences looking for relatives or any bits of information about family or friends. Once I pushed an aluminum dish through the wires. I should have known better; the current jolted me. But we heard that at night, when the lights were on the towers and the posts, to touch the wires with just one finger would electrocute a person instantly. I never saw anyone going to the wires to commit suicide, but I am sure that there were people who just couldn't take the suffering anymore. The fence provided a way out, to run to the wires and to end the suffering.

We knew Camp B as the "Czech Camp" since prisoners transported from Theresienstadt concentration camp in Czechoslovakia occupied it. One day, I saw an older man from the Czech camp standing by the fence holding a woolen scarf; a woman from my camp, holding a half ration of bread, bargained with him. After they agreed on the trade, the man threw the scarf to her, but it caught on the electrified wires. As he reached out to get his scarf, his right hand touched the wire. He screamed out in pain, but could not free his hand. Slowly, he lifted his left hand, placed it carefully between the wires, and pried his fingers loose one by one. With his hand free, he ran away, leaving the scarf behind.

Another time, I saw a group of women standing in a circle. I pushed closer to see what was going on; a young girl performed acrobatic exercises. As we watched her, we forgot for a few minutes where we were and how hungry we felt. Someone gave her a bite of bread for her little performance.

Once, I heard beautiful singing coming from the SS living quarters. A woman prisoner sang under their window. She had been a famous opera singer in Budapest. She sang in the hope that one of the SS officers would hear her and reward her with something to eat. After several songs, a door opened. An SS woman came out and gave her a piece of bread, yelling, "Take this and go away. Don't come back or you will be in big trouble." The opera singer thanked her and ran away. She never sang there again.

On another occasion, a woman who worked in the kitchen came up to me. She had a little piece of bread in her hand. "Are you Shabtai Slomovits' daughter from Chust?" she asked me.

"Yes, I am. Who are you?" I said.

"It is not important who I am. I knew your father, and he once did a big favor for my family." She gave me the bread and disappeared into the crowd of prisoners.

I never identified her or learned how she recognized me, but I discovered that my father's goodness reached me even here. I had not seen my father since the day we arrived in Auschwitz when the men were separated from the women.

In the last week of July 1944, the Nazis separated me from my mother and sister. They sent me to the Czech camp adjacent to Camp C, but I was still able to see and talk to them through the fence every day.

One morning, I met Lilly at the fence. She wore no shirt and covered herself with her arms, crying hopelessly.

"Lilly, what happened to you? Where is your shirt?" I asked.

"Someone stole it while I was washing myself at the water pipe. What will I do now?" she cried.

"Wait here," I told her. "I'll see what I can find." I had no idea what to do. All I knew was that my big sister was crying, cold, and scared. I wandered around the camp talking to the other prisoners, asking for help; a woman pointed out the clothing storage area where piles of clothes, stripped from the arriving prisoners, filled the barrack.

I lingered around this area, waiting for an opportunity to get nearer to the clothes. When no SS guards or Kapos were around, I sneaked in, snatched the first piece of clothing I saw, and ran out. I did not stop running until I reached Lilly at the fence.

She was still crying, covering her body. I looked at the rumpled cloth in my hand: a shirt! I pushed it carefully through the fence. "Here, Lillykeh, don't cry. And next time be more careful."

Birkenau, the main storage camp in Auschwitz, contained mountains of clothes, shoes, luggage, eyeglasses, pots and pans, sacks of shorn hair, books, and toys—the last possessions taken from over a million Jews who were killed at Auschwitz.

Every prisoner dreamed of being sent to work in Birkenau because of the possibilities for organizieren. One day, the guards sent me and a group of thirty other women to Birkenau for the day to load giant bundles of clothes onto trucks destined for Germany. We worked hard, but I preferred it to spending endless days languishing in the camp.

On our way back to the Czech camp, I passed a mountain of shoes. With winter approaching, the temperature was dropping. I looked down at my own worn shoes; I did not have much time to think. Quickly, I grabbed two shoes and hid them under my shirt. Just then, they ordered us to march back to our camp.

"Where are you from?" the prisoners from Birkenau called out to us as we marched past them. We were always thirsting for any information about our relatives—who was still alive, who was sent away from Auschwitz, who had heard any news.

"Do you know anyone from Munkacs, Chust, Solotfene?" a young woman asked me.

"Yes, I am from Chust," I said.

"Do you know Ella Heinfeld?" she asked.

"Yes, but . . ." and before I could reply, she pressed a pair of shoes into my hands. Now I was carrying two pairs of shoes.

"Please give these to Ella. Tell her they are from Magda, her cousin."

The SS and Kapos were pushing us along and shouting "Schnell!" (Quickly!) I did not have the chance to tell her that Ella, who was pregnant, had been taken away yesterday with all the other pregnant women. I hid the shoes under my skirt.

Now I had a dilemma. Magda had given me a pair of shoes for someone who no longer existed. Returning them to her was impossible, for I had already left her far behind.

My heart pounded as we approached the gate. The two pairs of shoes bulged under my clothes. Will the SS search me? What will they do to me if they find the shoes? Will they beat me? Will they kill me? As it turned out, they did not search me; this was my lucky day.

Arriving at my barrack, I took out the treasure I had snatched from the pile; a pair of mismatched men's shoes—one shoe was size ten, the other size eleven. Although I wore a size five, it did not matter. These shoes would keep my feet dry and warm during the coming winter. Flannel lined the other pair of shoes that Magda had given me, and they had a modern zipper in place of laces. I gave them to my mother so she could slip them on quickly when ordered to run outside for Appell. I had no shoes for Lilly.

One day, I was talking to Petyu Kreindler, a girl from my hometown, and as always, we talked about food. We came up with a plan for organizing some extra food.

We sewed two small sacks out of pieces of cloth from our dresses. Petyu had a pot with a handle. Late at night, when everyone was sleeping, we slipped out of our barrack and crept along the walls, praying that the guards would not see us.

We got to the kitchen area and waited in the darkness. We heard trucks approaching. They came every night dumping large mounds of vegetables onto the ground; prisoners carried the potatoes, carrots, and turnips into the kitchen. Petyu and I stood ready. The moment they left the vegetables unguarded, Petyu grabbed a potful of potatoes, ran back to me and emptied them into the sack. Then it was my turn to run, grab a potful of potatoes, and bring them to Petyu. We repeated this several times until we filled both our sacks.

We returned to our barrack and divided up the potatoes

evenly. Although we had little time left for sleeping, the potatoes and the hope of trading them for extra bread the next day compensated for the loss of sleep.

The next morning I walked to the fence of the men's camp. The old-timers had a small stove for cooking there. A man traded a loaf of bread for my potatoes, and I had to be very careful not to get electrocuted and not to be spotted by the SS as I passed the sack of potatoes through the fence.

I divided my loaf of bread evenly into three parts and hid them under my clothes until I saw my mother and sister waiting on the other side of the fence. Avoiding contact with the wires, I passed the two portions of bread through the fence to them.

The very thought that I could lessen their hunger and my own gave me the strength to continue doing this every night until I left Auschwitz.

8 Selections

"He is coming! He is coming!" The news had rumbled through the camp like a thunder clap. During selections prior to July 1944, my mother, my sister, and I held onto each other tightly.

In Auschwitz, they called Dr. Mengele "the Angel of Death," but by 1944, we just said, "He is coming!" Everyone knew who he was, and he came two or three times a week.

We ran to line up. Mengele's coming meant selections, and he chose people for different purposes, separating families and friends. What will the selection be for this time? Will he pick people to leave Auschwitz for slave labor in factories all over Europe? Will he choose pregnant women for medical experiments? Will he select the pretty girls and send them to the soldiers on the front? Will he ask those who play piano to step forward and then assign them to latrine duty? Will he choose the weak and sickly and send them to the gas chambers? We never knew, but we were always afraid.

Auschwitz had four crematoria. Even though I came from a small town, we had a crematorium in Chust. Cremating is against the Jewish religion, but non-Jewish people from the surrounding area who wanted their loved ones cremated came to our town. So when I came to Auschwitz and heard the word crematorium, I knew exactly what it was. They stood so high that no matter where you were in Auschwitz and Birkenau, if you looked in that direction, you could see the chimneys. While I was there in the summer months, when the Hungarian Jews arrived, the chimneys smoked constantly; sometimes flames flickered out the top. The gas chambers killed the people, and the crematoria burned the corpses.

Whenever Mengele came to our camp, a group of SS officers and soldiers accompanied him. He stood in front of the long rows of prisoners, and silently with a pointer in his gloved hand he indicated right, left, right, left. He did not have to say much; the Kapos and Blockaeltestes knew what to do.

Sometimes they conducted selections while we were dressed. Usually, this meant that Mengele would pick people to work in other labor camps or other parts of Auschwitz, but many times they ordered us to stand naked. Then Mengele chose the sickly looking people, the very skinny ones, and the ones with rashes or sores on their bodies. He checked our bodies quickly—a few red dots on the skin meant a death sentence. We knew that the order to undress meant that many of us would be torn from our families forever.

The first time I stood naked in Auschwitz two months earlier, I felt helpless and degraded, but with time I grew numb to this humiliating procedure. There was no other way.

One day, while standing naked in line, Mengele touched me with his gloved hand by moving my arm to see if I had a rash on my stomach. His touch felt like my doctor's touch back home—gentle and kind. He smiled faintly, but his smile was the smile of death. My skin was clear; he allowed me to stay with my mother and sister.

Another week went by. Mengele selected more people, but we were still together. The constant fear of separation filled us with panic whenever the "Angel of Death" came to our camp.

One time he asked all the women who were twins to step forward. I looked at my mother, not knowing what to do. I was a twin; my twin brother had died at the age of two. My mother was also a twin; her brother had also died in infancy. We heard the announcement, but without saying a word to each other, we did not move, maybe because my sister Lilly was there. Later, we heard about Mengele's terrible medical experiments on twins: he wanted to know how a German woman could have twins instead of one child. Very few of the twins the Nazis experimented on survived.

I know some stories that I still cannot share, but I'll share one. One day in Auschwitz, we were walking around. We didn't see any children because the Nazis killed them all when they arrived. Suddenly, we saw a young woman with a baby in her arms. We crowded around her asking, "How is it that you have a baby here?" She told us that she arrived in Auschwitz with her triplets, and right away Mengele took them from the train station for his "experiments." Only this baby survived. As I looked at the infant in amazement, I noticed a tattoo on her tiny arm. I never saw them again. This picture of the little child with a number tattooed on her arm will never leave me.

Three months after our arrival in Auschwitz, during the last week of July 1944, the dreaded day came. Dr. Mengele visited us again. Mother, Lilly, and I were holding onto each other. Mengele was looking for young women, sixteen to forty years old. I was sixteen years old, and Lilly was twenty; Mother was forty-three.

The guards lined up the women prisoners: five to a row, a thousand women in a column. Each line stepped up to Mengele. He looked and pointed—right or left. Our line approached him. He pointed: Mother to the left, Lilly and I to the right. Because we had not been ordered to undress, we knew that the women selected would be sent to work at another camp.

My heart was pounding so fast I thought it would leap out of my body. What should we do? What will happen to Mother? We cannot leave her alone.

Lilly looked at me and then quickly stepped out of our line and into the other line, next to Mother. I waited a few minutes, and when I thought no one was looking, I also sneaked into the other line. Suddenly, someone grabbed me from behind, slapped me hard on the face, and pushed me back into the right line. I met the eyes of the SS officer; he pointed to his rifle. I knew what he meant: You better stay put. You will not get a second chance.

The selection ended; they took me away. Mother and Lilly went back to their barrack. We waved and cried until we lost sight of each other.

I went through another Entlausung—sprayed from head to toe with a strong disinfectant. Then they took me to another camp in Auschwitz to await a work assignment.

The next day I discovered that I was in the camp next to Mother and Lilly, and I was able to see and talk to them once or twice a day. I stayed in this camp, which had conditions similar to the last one, for two and a half months.

In August, a group of freshly shaven, freshly dressed women came into my barrack. They looked clean and so much better than we did. I looked at them and thought, poor women, they don't know where they are. The next day, the whole group was taken away. Later, I learned that these were probably the women on Schindler's list.[1] Schindler's workers were taken to Auschwitz, but he asked for them back, and they all survived.

---

1. Oskar Schindler saved the lives of more than 1,000 Polish Jews during the Holocaust by requesting Jews in Auschwitz for work in his factory.

9 Tattoo

Somehow, in all the misery of Auschwitz we always knew the dates and holidays of the year, but we never knew the time of day. Through the prisoners' grapevine we also heard news about the war, but we never knew if it was the truth, propaganda, or just rumors.

Separated from my mother and sister, lying on the bunk bed in my barrack, I thought of the coming day—my birthday. What will this day bring me? Maybe a miracle will happen, I will wake up at home, and Auschwitz will be just a nightmare. I looked at my surroundings, and I knew it was not home. I prayed for sleep and perhaps a comforting dream to escape the misery, if only for a few hours, but my nagging hunger brought me back to the horrible present. Finally, I fell into a fitful sleep.

The next morning, we went through the usual routine—standing in line for the latrine and then standing for hours for Appell. The rest of the morning we just lingered around aimlessly with our constant hunger. We had no work to do to help pass the endless hours. Suddenly, we heard shouting, "Line up! Fast! Everybody move!"

As we ran to line up, a strange thing happened. The Blockaelteste stood in front of us and yelled, "Today you must line up single file in alphabetical order, according to last names. Quickly!" We all looked at each other in amazement. My last name started with an "S," so I joined the back of the line.

"What is happening? We always used only our first names here. What does it matter what our last names are?" I asked the girl standing next to me.

No one knew what was going on. We could not talk as we had to rush and obey orders. The Blockaelteste started to shout again, "Now we will go to the other side of the camp. Stay in alphabetical order. Move, quickly!"

A group of old-timers sat at tables waiting for us, two women per table: one woman had a big book open, and she was writing. The other woman sat next to her, and she had something in her hand. I stood far back in line and could not see what they were doing. As we approached the table, they asked us our full names and countries of origin. One of the women wrote a name down and dictated a number to the other woman who held an instrument in her hand that looked like a fountain pen with blue ink in it and an injection needle at the end. By the time I was close enough to see what was going on, I realized what was happening—they were tattooing our arms. Earlier, we had seen old-timers with numbers on their forearms: some on the outside of their arms, some on the inside of their arms, some large, and some small. We didn't know why.

When I first saw what they were going to do to us, I felt furious. They took away my family, they took away my belongings, and they took away my hair. They keep me cold, hungry, and miserable, and now they are going to put a number on my arm, just as though they were branding a cow. I felt so humiliated.

After a long wait, my turn came up.

"What is your name and where are you from?" the first woman asked me.

"Edith Slomovits from Chust, Hungary, which used to be Czechoslovakia before the war," I answered.

She wrote it down and dictated a number to the other girl. Then she grabbed my left arm and started to poke my skin with the strange instrument. With little stings, the needle pierced my skin, injecting blue ink until the inside of my arm read A-13215.

While this woman worked on my arm, I felt so overwhelmed with thoughts that I did not feel the pain. I am getting a number, and from now on I will be A-13215. I will not be able to switch from one barrack to another; the Germans will have a permanent record of where I am and where I should be. They are dehumanizing me. I will not be a person anymore, only a number. This upset me very much, but I couldn't afford to be upset because it wouldn't help me; nobody could help me.

Then other thoughts overtook me. I had to find a way to go on, so I tried to find something positive. If the Germans bother to give me a tattoo number, then they must have some plans for me—some living plans. To send me to the gas chamber, they don't need a number. Perhaps they will send me away to work—away from this hell called Auschwitz. I am not going to die here!

After they finished tattooing me, I did not feel humiliated at all. I felt hopeful. I will live! They could not take away my will to live. They could not take away my human dignity. As long as I am alive, I am a human being.

My arm healed in a few days, and the number was there forever. It was August 18th, 1944—my seventeenth birthday.

10 Sundays

Sundays in Auschwitz in Camp B were different from the rest of the week. We stood Appell only once, in the morning, and the guards made no selections on Sundays. These small changes from the usual routine made all the difference to us, and we waited for Sunday all week long.

The meager meals were the same as always. After the morning Appell, we milled around aimlessly outside or returned to our barracks and lay on our bunk beds.

In the late afternoon, after we devoured our daily rations, we remained outside. Thousands of us went to the fences to talk to relatives and friends on the other side. I went to the fence to talk to my mother and Lilly; we stood as close as possible to each other without touching the high voltage wires, which could instantly electrocute us. We shouted to be heard because the Sunday crowds on both sides of the fence grew even larger than on weekdays. We felt safer going to the fences on Sundays because fewer SS guards watched us then than during the rest of the week.

We could not bear the shouting, crying, and pushing. Thousands of women on both sides of the fence—like two human walls—tried to comfort and give hope to each other.

One day, while I was waiting for my mother and sister, I overheard a conversation between two girls standing on either side of the fence.

"Who is left from your family?" one girl asked.

"Just the two of us. Me and my good humor," the other girl answered with a sad smile.

Hearing this good-natured remark gave me the impetus to go on; I always wanted to hear and believe in the positive.

Suddenly, a shot rang out. We stood startled for a few seconds, and then everyone ran away. As I ran, I looked back but could not see what had happened. Later, I heard that the guards shot a woman to death on our side of the fence. The prisoners talked about this incident for a few days, but the next Sunday we were all at the fence again.

Again, we talked and shouted to each other and again, without warning, a shot rang out. The guards killed another young woman; everyone standing around the fallen woman ran away. I looked around to find out where the shot came from, but I did not see any SS guards. Then I looked up and saw an SS soldier in the guard tower aiming his rifle at us.

This random killing of a prisoner occurred repeatedly every Sunday. I knew that the same SS guard in the tower was shooting prisoners, entertaining himself on a Sunday afternoon.

One Sunday, in early September of 1944, I stood at the fence talking to my mother and Lilly. Gitta Salamon, Lilly's friend, who was also talking to her mother on the other side, stood next to me. All of a sudden, I heard a high-pitched sound; it was so close, so loud, that for a moment I thought the guards shot me. I jumped back, and then I saw Gitta lying on the ground. I felt as if I were meant to be the target that Sunday because I stood much closer to the fence than she did. Gitta's mother saw Gitta shot to death. I ran away as fast as I could, and I never stood so close to the fence again.

The picture of Gitta lying on the ground and her mother
fainting on the other side has never left me.

11 My Last Day In Auschwitz

The morning Appell ended, and we were standing outside the barracks when I heard someone yelling, "Mengele is coming!"

"What does he want today?" we asked each other. "What will his selections be for this time?"

"Line up! Fast!" the shouting began. We ran to line up—thousands of women in single file—ready for Mengele's inspection.

Mengele reached our group with his assistant officers and the Blockaelteste. As always, he wore his immaculate white gloves and carried a small pointer in his hand. Everyone was silent as he pointed right and left: healthy, strong women to the right; weak, sickly women to the left.

Right and left, right and left went the pointer. We stood in our designated groups for a long time until Mengele left our camp; then, all the women on the left side returned to the barracks.

The four hundred women selected for the right side, including myself, remained standing outside. Seeing the healthier looking women around me, I knew we would be sent to work somewhere; I prayed we would leave Auschwitz. Even though I did not know what was going on in the outside world or in other concentration camps, I believed that any place must be better than Auschwitz.

How was I going to reach my mother and sister and let them know that I was picked to go away? There was no possibility of reaching them because the guards ordered us to leave immediately.

"This group, let's go! Fast! March!" the Blockaelteste yelled.

They took us to the Entlausung building where they gave us our second cold shower since our arrival in May, five months before. They sprayed us with disinfectant powder and gave us different clothing: one pair of underwear, one dress, and a coat. What a treat this coat was. It was also another sign that we were going away to work.

Dressed in our "new" clothes, our march to the train began—a train that would bring us to a new destination, hopefully a better one. We left our camp and reached the main road of Auschwitz—the same road that had brought us here a few months ago.

The remaining prisoners stood by the fences watching us leave. As we marched, I searched their faces hoping to see someone who knew my mother and sister so that I could send a message to them, letting them know that I had left Auschwitz. But we had to march quickly, and there was no time for any communication with these prisoners.

Suddenly, from the corner of my eye, I saw someone running alongside of me on the other side of the fence, a little woman trying hard to keep up with us; I looked again and recognized my mother. Nobody was outside in Camp C—only my mother. It was a miracle seeing her at this crucial moment. We tried to talk to each other quickly.

"Mother, where is Lilly?" I shouted.

"She left Auschwitz yesterday," my mother answered.

"Where did she go?"

"I don't know. Mengele was here, and he selected a group of

young women. I hope she left for a work camp."

I marched; my mother ran. We tried to say goodbye. We tried to promise each other that our family would reunite one day, but we could not. We were choking with tears. I looked back at my mother as long as I could, not knowing when or if I would ever see her again. We reached the gate—a last wave, a last kiss in the air—and we were separated from each other.

I left Auschwitz with the knowledge that my mother was left alone there as an "older" person at 43—Lilly and I were leaving—and I was sure that they would kill her. For the rest of the year, I cried for my mother. I cried so much at that time that I used up all of my tears for a lifetime.

Outside the camp on the main road, a long cattle train waited for us. We stopped and waited for the order to board. I turned around to look at Auschwitz for the last time when I heard a voice calling. I did not see anyone, and I did not know where the sound was coming from.

"Help me! Help me!" The voice became louder.

Then I saw a small face peering out the cellar window of a large, concrete building. The window had iron bars on it, and inside the cellar hundreds of women were locked up like animals in a cage. I moved closer to the window and saw a young girl my age, crying and asking for help. I tried to talk to the girl but did not know what to say; there was nothing I or anyone else could do. I knew that these women in the cellar would never get out. Their fate was the gas chamber.

Many hours had passed since we left Camp B. Still waiting for permission to sit down, we felt exhausted. The old-timers and the SS counted us over and over again. Additional SS officers arrived and started talking to the Blockaelteste and Kapos in charge of our group. The talking turned into an argument. We did not hear what they were saying, but we could see the Blockaelteste gesturing angrily and not giving in to the demands of the SS. The arguing went on for a long time; finally, they told us to board the train.

Inside the cattle car, we sat on the bare floor in complete

darkness, but the train did not move. We waited for several more hours. One of the old-timers came into our car and told us what happened.

The SS officers in charge of the gas chambers had extra room for a few hundred more women. When they saw our group standing in line for the train, they wanted to take us to fill up the gas chambers; luckily, the Blockaelteste and her helpers did not give in to their demands. They argued with the SS, telling them that our group was destined for a factory in Germany. They knew that if they did not deliver the specified number of women, they would have to pay with their own lives. This time, these old-timers saved our lives.

All of a sudden, the camp sirens sounded, and we heard explosions—one after another. We thought the Americans were bombing Auschwitz. I felt very scared, but after our narrow escape from the gas chambers, I believed that the bombing would not harm us. Then it was quiet.

After several more hours of waiting, the train began to move. We left Auschwitz!

After the war I heard that on the night of October 7, 1944, the night I left Auschwitz, the explosions I heard were not from American bombers. That night, prisoners revolted in Auschwitz. Over the course of several months, a group of male prisoners had managed to smuggle in explosives from the munitions factory where they worked. Secretly, they had built bombs and planned the revolt. On that night they destroyed two crematoria and killed several SS guards; some of the prisoners escaped. The Germans killed those whom they caught, but the bravery of the prisoners slowed down the monstrous German killing machine.

12 Sabotage

We left Auschwitz in October 1944 and transferred to the village of Taucha, near Leipzig, Germany. In Taucha there was a small labor camp of about 1,200 people from all over Europe: about 400 Jewish men, 400 Jewish women, 200 gypsy women, and 200 women who were criminals or political prisoners. The conditions in Taucha were much better than in Auschwitz—any camp was better than Auschwitz—and we felt lucky to have been sent there.

The barracks were small—thirty people per room, all Jewish women in mine. Each prisoner had her own bed, blanket, and straw to sleep on. The room also had lights, which we used in the evening when we came back from work.

The food was better, and we received a bit more. They fed us twice daily. At noon we got a bowl of vegetable soup with little pieces of meat in it. The evening meal consisted of two slices of bread, one slice of salami, and a small square of margarine, but we were still hungry all the time.

A male prisoner twice my size received the same amount of food as I. When I saw how hungry the men were, I thought of my father and brother. Are they so hungry too? Are they so miserable? If they were only here with me, I would try to help them. The only "good" that came from the separation of my family was that we did not have to see each other suffering.

We worked around the clock in twelve-hour shifts in a large weapons factory an hour's walk from the camp. We went to work at either 5:00 a.m. or 5:00 p.m.; the sky was always dark no matter when we started. They alternated our shifts every week.

We marched to the factory in a long column, five people to a row. Not too many SS guards watched us. It would have been easy to step out of line and disappear. It crossed my mind every day, but where would I go? If I managed to escape to the village or to the countryside, I would be instantly recognized by my odd clothing and shaved head. No German would have helped me; an escape would have been sure suicide.

We preferred to work on the day shift. That shift slept at night and received two meals during the working hours. The night shift prisoners worked for twelve hours without getting any meals. They returned to camp at 6:00 a.m., tired and hungry, and went straight to sleep. The SS woke them at noon to receive their mid-day soup. After this meal, they went back to sleep and had to get up again at 4:00 p.m. to wash, get their evening meal, and go to work. As hungry as they were, they tried to save some bread for the long, twelve-hour stretch at night.

The factory manufactured the Panzer Faust—an anti-tank missile. I worked on the welding machines. On each machine a thin metal rod protruded from its side. Two girls sat on either side of the rod. On the rod we fit a pipe onto which we welded a small metal plate. In order to weld the plate to the pipe, we had to push a foot pedal eleven times, simultaneously adjusting the pipe with both hands. Both the pipe and plate had three holes; we had to match the holes exactly. If they mismatched even a fraction of a millimeter, the pipe was useless. It had to be taken to another department where it was dismantled and reassembled.

The unwelded pipes were stacked at the side of the machine. One of the male prisoners supplied the workers at the machine with the metal plates. Each time he gave us fifty plates, he made a chalk mark on the side of the machine.

In the beginning, each team of girls made approximately 600 pieces a day. The German foreman pushed for more, and the girls strained harder and harder. After several weeks, each team was producing 1,000 units in a twelve-hour shift, but the SS wanted even more. They promised us a bonus—extra food—for the girls who produced the most units. Many girls overexerted themselves, desperately trying to earn the extra food. By the end of the second month, many girls were making 1,500 units a day, and this became the norm. I was not one of these girls.

One day, I watched the male prisoner marking the machines with hatch marks to indicate how many units were being made. Secretly, I got hold of a piece of chalk and added some marks of my own whenever he was not looking; many times, even my partner did not know what I was doing. Using this secret method, I added 300 to 400 non-existent units per day. By the time the shifts ended, I felt elated that I had "produced" so many units. Every time I added a chalk mark, I felt I was shortening the war and fighting the Nazis.

Once, during the night shift, I almost fell asleep at the machine. I sensed the German foreman staring at me, and I started to work faster.

"I don't like the way you work," he said to me. "You do not produce as much as the other girls."

I felt the blood draining from my face as I looked up at him. What is he going to do to me? He looked at me—a small, skinny, terrified, 17-year-old girl—for a long time.

"From now on I will keep you on the day shift, but you must produce 1,000 units per day," he said sternly. "If not, I will report you to the SS."

I could not believe my ears. I will be one of the lucky ones who works on the day shift all the time. I will be able to sleep all night, I will have my food during the waking hours, and I will not have to save any bread for the night. This was the best thing that could happen to me at the time.

"Thank you, thank you! I promise I will work harder," I answered quickly before he could change his mind.

After several days on the day shift, I resumed my secret method and added chalk marks to "increase" my production.

For several weeks my partner at the machine was a girl from Budapest. As we worked, we played a game to help pass the time. We fantasized that after the war we would visit each other, and we imagined what food we would serve in our homes. She would serve me delicious Hungarian dishes—chicken paprikash, veal goulash, and for dessert a rich, chocolate torte. I would make her a traditional Sabbath meal of gefilte fish, chicken soup, kugel, chopped liver, cholent,[1] and tzimmes.[2] We went on and on with all the dishes we remembered from home; the game did not make us less hungry, but it gave us hope.

When I watched the girls straining to produce the maximum amount of units, I tried to talk to them.

"What are you doing? Why are you pushing yourself to make more and more? Do you realize that you push that foot pedal 16,500 times a day? Don't you see that you are making more ammunition for the Germans, and this will only prolong the war? Don't you want to go home?"

They looked at me with sad eyes, turned away, and did not answer. The bonus, the extra food that was promised to them, blinded them to everything else.

When I realized that I could not convince them and that I could only act alone, I started sabotaging in another way. Cautiously, I mismatched the holes of the metal plate with the holes of the pipe.

But, there was a time when I had misgivings. They gave out

---

1. A stew simmered over a low flame for many hours and served by Jews on Shabbat (Sabbath).
2. Jewish cuisine of various sweetened combinations of vegetables, fruit, and sometimes meat, prepared as a casserole.

the bonus. It was a whole herring, and I did not get one, for I was known as a poor worker. For a moment, I thought, maybe I was wrong. I could have had a herring. But then I found my answer. For one herring, should I prolong the war? No! I did the right thing. As it turned out, they never gave out another bonus.

One day an officer from the Wehrmacht (the German Army), who was an expert on the Panzer Faust, came to inspect our factory. A good missile could destroy a tank, but one with even the smallest defect would miss the target. The officer spoke to the foreman in German, which I spoke fluently.

"Who is sabotaging in this factory?" he shouted. "Many of the Panzer Fausts are not performing. They explode before they reach the target. Many go off target completely!"

He went on and on. My heart pounded wildly; I wanted to shout out, "I am doing it! I am fighting the Nazis!" But I continued to work quietly.

When a pipe was ready, we put it on a conveyor belt and sent it to the next department. No one could tell who made the pipe once we put it on the belt. The Wermacht officer stood at the head of the conveyor belt, checking every pipe. When he saw that it was impossible to detect who was sabotaging, he came up with an idea; he ordered a little device to be put on every machine that numbered each pipe before it went on the conveyor belt. The new system scared me. I would not be able to sabotage by mismatching anymore. I could still make fewer pieces, but I would no longer be able to make defective ones, and I would have to be extremely careful.

One day, the German foreman told us, without much explanation, that the numbering devices did not work. He took them off the machines. From that day on until our evacuation from the camp, I made more bad pipes than good ones.

I resisted the Nazis, but I was not alone. Whether it was intentional sabotage or quiet suffering, it was resistance. Not giving in to the hunger and cold, not breaking down from the grueling work, enduring every imaginable pain, anguish, and torture—that was resistance. Every one of us who survived—and many who did not—resisted.

13 The Gypsies

One of the groups of prisoners in Taucha consisted of two hundred young Gypsy women from all over Europe.

The Gypsies, regardless of their country of origin, spoke a common language, Romany. Most of them came from wandering tribes who traveled in wagons from town to town making a living from fortune telling, cleaning outhouses, and other jobs. The other Gypsies came from the big cities: Berlin, Prague, Budapest, and Bucharest. They performed professionally as dancers, singers, acrobats, and musicians; they were more sophisticated than the others.

The Nazis transferred the Gypsy women to Taucha at the same time that we arrived, but only they arrived wearing striped prisoners' clothing. The rest of their families were left behind in Auschwitz never to be seen again.

As in Auschwitz, men, women, and Gypsies lived in separate camps, but unlike Auschwitz, electricity did not charge the barbed wire that separated the camps in Taucha.

At the factory, we all worked together and could talk to one another. When I first met the Gypsies, I was friendly to them, and we exchanged information about ourselves.

Some of the male prisoners had contact with German officers and civilians when they did extra work for them. In exchange, they received cigarettes.

Many of the Gypsy women traded their bread for cigarettes. After the women finished smoking their precious cigarettes, they still felt hungry. With nothing left to trade but their bodies, they slept with the male prisoners for a piece of bread. This was very risky, for guards sent prisoners caught together to a death camp.

A few days before New Year's Eve of 1945, I heard, with surprise, from my fellow prisoners that there would be a performance put on for us in the camp. The SS ordered the Gypsies to prepare a show, and the excitement grew great. It seemed unbelievable because we had already forgotten about such things as shows and entertainment.

On the day of the performance, they took us to the dining area. All the women prisoners sat on the ground. The Gypsy girls danced, sang, and performed acrobatics, and they made us forget, for a little while, where we were. I felt so grateful to them that afterwards I went up to the performers and thanked them.

I particularly remember a beautiful young Gypsy girl from Berlin: tall with straight, black hair, large, dark eyes, and a charming smile. Somehow, she obtained a top hat and a cane. She entertained us with a lively singing and tap dance act. She was full of energy, and I could have watched her dance for hours. But after the show, life went back to the same bleak routine.

Several weeks after the performance, one of the older Gypsy women at the factory pushed me roughly for no reason.

"Why did you push me?" I asked her. "What did I do to you?"

"You dirty Jew!" she yelled at me. "Because of you, I am here in this camp."

"Because of me?" I asked, surprised by her response. "I am as miserable here as you are. Why is it my fault?"

"Because you Jews caused the war, and because of the war, I am here!" she screamed.

By this time, a big crowd had gathered around us. The Jewish prisoners looked on in silent shock as the Gypsies and other non-Jewish prisoners joined in the yelling.

"I did not cause the war. Hitler did," I said.

"No, Hitler said the Jews made the war, and he was right. Everything is your fault."

I tried to reason with her, but it was impossible. I walked away crying, not understanding how I, a seventeen-year-old girl, could have caused this terrible war.

From that day on, I kept my distance from the Gypsies.

14 The Gray Woolen Socks

Early one morning in the infirmary at Taucha, I woke up and looked out the window. Snow fell in the bitter cold outside, and in the infirmary it was dark and quiet. I could see figures rushing in and out of one of the small barracks where the toilets and cold water faucets were; the prisoners were getting ready to go to work. As the darkness started to fade, I recognized many of their tired faces.

For the moment, I felt secure in the warm room where I had been for the past three weeks, but I knew that in another day or two I would be sent back to work.

It is hard to believe that there was an infirmary in a labor camp, but the Nazis needed us in relatively good condition so that we could work in their munitions factory. The infirmary consisted of a large room with a small entry hall. Twenty beds, two rows of ten, lined the walls, and a little stove stood in the middle of the room for heating. The only medical instrument in the infirmary was a thermometer.

A young Ukrainian prisoner named Maria served as our nurse. She was anti-Semitic and showed favoritism to her own people; she made sure that there were always more non-Jewish women in the infirmary than Jewish ones even though we outnumbered them two to one. She enforced strict discipline and never hesitated to strike the Jewish prisoners in her care. She had the power to help or harm us, and Maria terrified me.

The camp's one doctor, a Hungarian Jew and inmate, served all 1,200 prisoners. He showed compassion for every person, and his kindness gave much support to the sick.

In a small room in the infirmary, the doctor examined the prisoners. If the thermometer indicated fever and the doctor could determine an illness which required rest, he sent the prisoner to the infirmary, but to report sick was very risky as the Germans often sent the sick back to Auschwitz or other death camps. When the Nazis sent someone away, we never saw that person again.

December arrived, and the days became colder. My large, mismatched men's shoes wore out, and I had no socks. I did not even have rags to wrap around my feet to keep the snow out of my shoes. I developed a cough, and every evening I felt feverish and extremely tired. My friends urged me to see the doctor, but I was afraid. I was not getting better; finally, I summoned up my courage and went to see him.

"You have a fever, my child, but it may go away," he told me as he listened to my lungs. "Try to stay indoors as much as possible, and if you do not feel better in a few days, come to see me again."

"But, Herr Doctor, you won't send me away from Taucha, will you?" I asked.

"No, no. I will not let them send you away," he reassured me.

I went back to work, but my condition worsened. My fever rose, and I felt pain in my left shoulder. I went back to the doctor, and he told me that the top of my left lung was infected. He sent me to the infirmary; I felt so relieved not to have to return to work in this cold weather that I forgot about the possible risk of being in the infirmary. I appreciated the luxury of staying in a bed, in a warm room, and not having to get up at 4:30 in the morning.

In the infirmary, the nights were quiet, and the days started late. But we ate the same two daily meals that the working prisoners ate.

The nurse measured our temperatures daily. When patients recovered, the doctor released them, and others took their places. When patients died, the Nazis took them to other camps, as Taucha had no crematorium.

After a few days of rest, I started to walk around the room. All twenty beds were occupied by women of different ages and nationalities. We spoke several languages—Yiddish, Hungarian, Polish, Czech, French, Russian, and Romany—but we used broken German as our common language.

Every day, a bedridden French woman in her early forties asked me to toast her bread on top of the little stove.

"Very dark, almost burnt," she told me.

I gladly did it for her, and one day she surprised me by giving me a piece of toast for my help.

A Jewish girl in her twenties occupied the bed next to mine.

"What is your name?" I asked her in Yiddish.

"Zlate," she told me. We used only first names.

"Why are you here?" I asked her.

"I have syphilis," she answered simply.

"Syphilis!" I was shocked. Even at a young age, I knew of the seriousness of that disease. I had never heard of a Jewish girl getting syphilis. "How did you get it?"

"It happened before I was taken to concentration camp," she told me. "I had an affair with a man I hardly knew."

"Why did you do it?" I asked

"He told me he would marry me," she said quietly.

"And. . . ," I pressed her for more.

"I never saw him again." She fell silent and turned away from me; we never spoke about it again. I left the infirmary before Zlate did and never found out what happened to her.

Across from my bed, two Polish women in their early fif-
ties chattered loudly in Polish all day long, punctuating every
sentence with "Prosze Pani" (dear lady). I had to restrain myself
from shouting, "Shut up! Stop! Enough already!"

A young Gypsy girl who suffered from tuberculosis occupied
another bed. She died, and the Nazis took her away.

The next day a pretty, twenty-eight-year-old woman from
Hungary named Vera occupied her bed. In great pain, she came
in with a fever and an abscess on her leg. The doctor took one
look at her leg and said, "Vera, dear, this does not look good. I
must operate immediately to save your life. As you know, I have
no instruments, no anesthesia, and no medication."

The room fell silent, filled with tension. An operation, here?
How is it possible?

"I have a pocket knife. I can hypnotize you so that you will
feel no pain," he said. "If you agree, I will try this operation."

"Yes, yes, Herr Doctor," Vera said. "I agree to everything. I
want to live!"

The doctor placed the pocket knife on the stove to sterilize
it. He tied a string around a small stone to make a pendulum
and swung it back and forth in front of Vera's eyes; the hypnosis
began. We all held our breath, watching and praying. Slowly,
Vera closed her eyes. The doctor started to operate with the little
knife. She was very quiet, moaning softly in her sleep. Some
of us tore up our undershirts and made bandages for her. After
completing the surgery, the doctor bandaged her leg and woke
her up. She felt much better and did not remember anything. Vera
recuperated completely, and the nurse sent her back to work.

One evening, Maria, the prisoner-nurse, went out to meet one
of her friends returning from work. We could hear them talking
in the hallway. A few minutes later Maria returned to the main
room of the infirmary.

I got up to get a drink of water and wandered into the little
hallway. There, on the bench, I saw a pair of new gray woolen
knee socks. I knew that in a few days I would be discharged from
the infirmary and sent back to work in the cold. I had no socks,

and here I stood, with nobody around, looking at a pair of socks as if they were waiting for me. Should I take them? Who did they belong to? I hesitated, but I knew that if I did not take them, the next person coming by would. I needed the socks desperately. I do not know if I stood there for thirty seconds or thirty minutes, but finally I took the socks, hid them under my dress, and went back to bed. Once inside, I carefully tucked the socks under my straw mattress and did not tell anyone.

Maria went out again, but suddenly she burst back into the room yelling, "I had a pair of woolen knee socks outside. Who took them? No one answered. "I'm going to search everyone and God help the person who took them," she screamed.

I felt so scared that I did not know what to do. I would have given them back, but I knew that even if I returned the socks voluntarily, Maria would beat me. I lay in bed praying silently.

Maria continued screaming and then abruptly left the room. There was not a sound in the infirmary or the hallway. After a few seconds, she returned, holding a pair of new gray woolen socks.

"I found my socks," she said simply, closing the matter.

I looked at her socks. They were identical to the pair I had found. When the lights went out, I checked under my mattress, and I found my socks. But how did Maria get the other pair? There was no one in the hallway when she went out the second time, and no one had come in. Maria had her socks, and I had mine.

Two days later, the doctor discharged me from the infirmary. I put on my new socks and went back to work. The socks kept my feet warm and dry, and I wore them all winter until the end of the war.

The mystery of the socks puzzles me to this day. The only answer I have is that God provided this personal miracle for me.

15 Rachel's Siddur

She must have felt my stare. She lifted her eyes from the Siddur,[1] looked at me, but did not interrupt her prayers. When she finished, she came over to me.

"Would you like to say the Shmah?"[2] she asked me quietly.

"Yes, please," I said.

"What is your name?" she asked me.

"Edith. What is yours?"

"Rachel," she said in a friendly voice and handed me her cherished Siddur.

I took it in disbelief. A Siddur in my hands, in this place! I started to say the prayers. I felt afraid that someone would take the Siddur away, or worse yet, I would wake up from a dream.

Rachel watched me with a reassuring look. "It's all right; don't worry. Say your prayers."

I kissed the Siddur and handed it back to Rachel. I wanted to thank her, but she put her finger to her lips and nodded, "No."

---

1. A Jewish prayer book.
2. A Jewish prayer stating that God is One.

"Don't thank me, Edith. We all pray for the same things."

"How did you . . . Where did you get this Siddur?" I asked in amazement.

"I have had it for some time now," she answered evasively. "Whenever you want to pray, just come to me."

Later, I found out that she had "organized" this Siddur in Auschwitz (before we were transported to Taucha) by trading several of her daily portions of bread.

My God, I thought. How strong she must be to give up her bread. Bread meant life for every prisoner.

I saw Rachel whenever we were on the same work shift at the munitions factory. She always kept the Siddur with her, and she let me pray from it whenever I wanted. I wished I could do something for her, too.

One day, I saw Rachel carrying a big sack and her Siddur. We talked for a while. She gave me her Siddur, and I prayed silently. I asked her if there was anything I could do for her; she smiled and again evaded my question.

"Did you know that last week was Purim?"[3] Rachel asked.

"Yes," I answered, "and Passover is coming soon."

We were silent, each with our own thoughts—perhaps the same thoughts: Passover, the family, the Seder. . . .

"What do you think, Rachel? Will we be home for Passover?"

"How I wish that were so, but it does not seem like it," she answered.

"But the news is good. Maybe the war will end by then," I persisted.

"Yes, the news is good, but what do we really know? Only God knows the answer," she replied.

"God took the Jews out of Egypt. Couldn't He take us out

---

3. A Jewish holiday that celebrates the deliverance of the Jewish people from Haman's plot to annihilate them, as recorded in the biblical *Book of Esther*.

of here? Why are we here in the first place? Where is God?"
I pleaded.

"God is here," she said with quiet conviction. "You must not
lose hope."

Suddenly, I had a revelation. I forgot about everyone around
me; I felt as if I were standing before God alone, just God and
me. I realized that the answer was there from my very first
day in Auschwitz: God was not to blame. Instead, I blamed
the Germans for my being in a concentration camp, for being
separated from my family, for being so very hungry, cold, and
miserable. Once I understood this, I prayed to God to help me
out of this situation.

I looked back at Rachel's large and heavy bag and again
asked her what was in it. She told me that she was exchanging
some of her daily bread rations for carrots, squash, and other
vegetables so she would not have to eat bread during the eight
days of Passover.

"How do you make exchanges?" I asked.

"It's not easy. It takes time and patience, so I started early,"
she said.

Then I knew what I could do for her: I asked around and did
some organizieren for her and myself.

Passover arrived. A group of girls who did not have to go to
the night shift sat together in the barrack and had a Seder. Rachel
read some passages from her Siddur; some of the Passover bless-
ings we knew by heart. We did not sing; instead, we meditated in
silence. When we came to the last sentence of the Haggadah,[4] we
repeated over and over again: "Next year in Jerusalem. . . Next
year in Jerusalem. . . ." Whenever we will be liberated will be our
next year. Wherever we will be liberated will be our Jerusalem.

That night none of us ate bread. I did not touch bread for the
next twenty-four hours. Rachel stayed away from bread for the
entire eight days of Passover.

---

4. The book containing the Passover Seder service.

Five weeks after Passover, the Allies liberated us. I heard from a former camp inmate that Rachel survived and returned to her native Romania; she married a Chassid,[5] had several children, and lived a religious life.

5. An ultra-orthodox Jew.

16 Yossele

In Taucha, I met a Jewish man named Miklos who had with him his ten-year-old son, Yossele, a beautiful and bright boy—the only child in Taucha.

I often spoke to Miklos in the factory, and we became friends. He told me that when he arrived in Auschwitz, his wife and two younger children were sent to the left, to their death. But Dr. Mengele chose Yossele to be a Laufer—an errand boy. Mengele would pick out good-looking boys, dress them in white, and use them to run errands throughout the camp for the SS. When Mengele tired of these Laufers, he sent them to the gas chambers and chose other young boys from the new arrivals.

Somehow, Miklos managed to hide Yossele in Auschwitz after Mengele no longer needed him, and they arrived in Taucha together.

I saw Yossele several times in Taucha, but never in the factory; Miklos kept him hidden in the barrack until our evacuation started in April of 1945.

After the war, I met up with a fellow prisoner from Taucha. The first thing I asked him was, "How are Miklos and his little Yossele?"

He answered, "At the last minute, as the SS were jumping onto trucks to escape the advancing Russian army, they opened fire with their machine guns, killing as many prisoners as they could." He continued in a sad voice, "Miklos and his little Yossele were among the slaughtered."

I was speechless and started to cry. I wished I had never asked. I wished I had been left with my hope, my fantasy that somewhere, somehow, Miklos and his beloved Yossele had survived and were still together.

17 March to Freedom

By April of 1945, I had been in Auschwitz and Taucha for a year.

We noticed something different: a strange tension hung in the air. The night shift workers had returned, but the SS did not send the next shift, my shift, to the factory. We stood outside our barracks along with the night shift workers, waiting for the next order.

The guards ran around frantically. We knew the Germans were losing the war, and the end was near, but we did not know when, where, or how it would end. Every day seemed like an eternity. We looked at each other with questioning eyes, but no one had any answers.

Suddenly, the SS started to shout, "Raus, Schnell, Appell!" We lined up—five people to a row. We had no belongings, but some of us managed to run back into the barracks and grab a blanket from our bunks. We had no idea where we were going, but we prayed that the SS would not take us to another concentration camp.

They did not bother to count us, as they used to do so meticulously. They took up position, and with their rifles pointed at us, we evacuated the camp. The march began.

The first day we marched twenty-five miles without getting any food. In one place, we saw a burned down camp. The spring rain fell continuously. The ground was still frozen, but several men tried to find a few potatoes or vegetables in the ground. Although they were frozen, the men still ate them.

At nightfall, when we reached a forest—hungry, exhausted, and wet—the SS allowed us to sit and rest.

At dawn, before the Germans had a chance to line us up, we saw Allied planes fill the sky; the Germans panicked. They pushed us deeper into the forest and ordered us to lie flat on the ground. Somehow, I managed to crawl out into a clearing and watch the planes: bombs fell. I heard explosions all around me, but I was not afraid. I believed the Allies would never hurt me because I was not the enemy.

When the bombing stopped, our march continued. The road became wider and more populated. Three columns of people moved steadily.

We, the prisoners, walked in the first row, which included prisoners from other camps, all dressed shabbily, many of us without shoes, some of us with blankets thrown over our heads. The blankets were soaking wet, but it was better with them than without them.

A few scattered units of the German army—what was left of it—moved along next to us, in wagons and on foot.

In the third column were the German civilians, fleeing their homes before the approaching Russian army. Seeing the German army and the civilians running away gave me new strength to go on.

I felt even more optimistic when I read the writing on the village walls, "Wir werden nicht kapitulieren!" (We will not surrender!) The mere fact that the Germans used the word "surrender" proved to me that they considered that a possibility. What a difference this was from Hitler's earlier diatribes when he boasted about his military triumphs and his plans to conquer Europe and destroy the Jewish people. Over and over again, in every village, I saw, "Wir werden nicht kapitulieren!"

The war will be over soon, I thought. I will go home to my family. I will hug them and kiss them. I will eat bread and more bread and then some more. But right now I am still in the Germans' hands, and I must do everything possible to survive.

Cold and miserable, many of the girls marching next to me lacked blankets. The German wagons filled with soldiers, blankets, and other supplies rolled by. I looked around, making sure no one was watching, and grabbed a blanket from a moving wagon. I gave it to one of the girls in my row. I waited; nothing happened. I snatched another blanket from the next wagon and gave it to another girl. The German soldiers, too busy with their own troubles, paid no attention to me. Gradually, I supplied myself and the girls around me with dry military blankets.

We marched twenty to twenty-five miles a day. I felt exhausted and could barely walk when a new idea came to me. I jumped onto the back of a wagon and rode on it for a few miles.

"Edith, what are you doing? Come back here!" the girls shouted when they saw me riding on the wagon.

"Don't worry," I told them. "I'll wait for you."

"The SS will shoot you. Don't do it!"

"They won't notice me," I assured them.

I rode this way for a while and then hopped off the wagon and waited for my row of girls to catch up with me. When they arrived, I continued to walk with them. After a short while, I jumped on another wagon and rode a few more miles. It was very dangerous, but I conserved a lot of energy this way—energy that helped me survive.

We passed many village signs. The names were unfamiliar to me, but after several days, I started recognizing some of the names and realized that we were walking in a circle. The Germans were retreating, but whenever they thought they had reached a safe place, it was already occupied by the Allies.

We reached the Dresden area after marching in a circle for over two weeks—a circle that was becoming smaller and smaller each day. I knew this meant the war would end soon.

One day, we arrived in a village we had been to before. The villagers were running around in confusion.

Suddenly, I saw a familiar face, Magda Horvat, a gentile girl from my home town; we had been classmates for four years.

Our eyes met, but she did not recognize me, skinny and dirty, with tattered clothes. A wet blanket covered my head; I looked at her for a long time, not knowing what to do.

She is here in Germany, I thought. She had to run away from Chust. She was afraid of the Russians.

I wanted to ask her for some food, but in spite of my painful hunger, my pride would not let me. I did not want her to see me in my condition.

As I looked at her, I remembered the streets of Chust and how she had pretended not to recognize me because I was Jewish. I remembered how her parents took away my uncle's business and how her family moved into my grandparents' house.

When the SS deported us, she and other non-Jewish classmates of mine had sat behind a long table at the train station, checking our papers before the soldiers forced us to go through a humiliating body search. As they shoved us into the trains, Magda and her friends were laughing, not showing the slightest compassion for what they saw happening.

As I looked at her, memories of my family filled my mind—memories and questions. Where is my father? My mother? My sister? My brother? Are they alive? Are they free already? Are they as hungry as I am? But shouts from the SS guards to move on brought me back to reality, and without looking back at her I continued the march.

The next day, we arrived at a forest and stayed there for six days. Finally, the SS allowed us to sit down after days of walking. With the Allies closing in from all directions, there was nowhere else to go.

The relief did not last long, however, as hunger replaced fatigue. During the march the guards gave us only one piece of bread every three or four days. Some people lay on the wet ground, too weak to move on; others looked around to see if there were anything they could do to stay alive.

One day, I saw a group of prisoners crowd around something. I went to see what it was but could not get close enough. Everyone was pushing and shouting. I started to push also and when I got to the center of the crowd, I saw a dead horse lying on the ground. The prisoners were tearing off pieces of the carcass and eating it raw. Some prisoners used a piece of broken glass or a sharp rock; others ripped off the flesh with their bare hands. Someone offered me his makeshift knife, but I could not bring myself to eat from the dead horse.

As I wandered around the forest looking for something to eat, I heard a faint trickling sound and followed it through the woods and down a hill. There, I saw a long-forgotten sight—a small stream of clean, fresh water. The rain had stopped for a few hours, and the sun came out.

First, I took a long drink. It was so refreshing, so clean, so pure—like a taste of freedom. Then, I took off my dress and shoes and waded into the stream. There were several other girls there too. We washed ourselves, we drank the fresh water, and for the first time in a long time, we laughed. We felt new strength and courage returning to us.

If there is such a beautiful stream of fresh water, I thought, surely there must be other beautiful things in the world waiting for me. I felt so excited that I ran back to my group of girls to tell them about the stream.

"What happened to you?" they asked when I returned. "You look so clean, so happy, so different. What did you do? Where did you go?"

"I washed myself. I drank fresh, clean water, Mayim Chayim—life-giving water. Beyond the hill is a beautiful stream of the most delicious water in the world. Go down there, all of you. Have a drink and wash yourselves," I told them. But only one girl, Irene, had the strength to get up and join me; the others were too weak to move.

Back in the forest, many of the SS troops were running away from the approaching Allies. Some stayed, hoping the prisoners would not turn against them.

The SS Commandant of the women's camp at Taucha had always called us swine, vermin, lice—never human beings with names. But now, in the final stage of the war, she suddenly remembered our names and approached us.

"Joli, will you tell the Russians that I was good to you?" she asked.

"Yes, of course," Joli answered.

"Agi, will you tell them that I never hit you? Will you say that I gave you enough food?"

"Yes, yes, I will," she answered.

It was hard to believe that these Germans were asking for mercy from the very people they had tortured and abused. But they still had their guns, our fate was still in their hands, and we were still afraid.

Another two days passed without receiving any food. Because of the unbearable hunger, some of the prisoners sneaked into the villages to beg for food.

One day, three sisters slipped into the nearest village. Each sister went to a different house to ask for food. Before dark, only two of the sisters returned to the forest. The third never returned; she disappeared without a trace.

The next day two other sisters tried their luck in the same village, but before they reached the village, the SS shot at them.

Somehow, they managed to get back to the forest; both of them were bleeding heavily. The older sister had two bullet holes in her thighs. The younger girl was shot in the shin.

We rushed to find the Jewish doctor—a prisoner like the rest of us. He came and looked at both women and bandaged the younger one with a torn undershirt, but he could do little more. She bled to death while we looked on helplessly. We buried her there. The older sister recuperated and survived the war.

Another day passed, and the hunger did not subside. In spite of the other girls' tragedy, I decided to go into the village and find some food. I asked the girls if anyone would join me, but no one responded. They were afraid and warned me not to go, but my hunger overpowered all reasoning.

"Maybe it will be easier to die from a bullet than from hunger," I said. My mind was made up. Just as I said goodbye, Irene stood up; she was much taller and older than I was.

"Wait Edith, I'll go with you," she said.

We arrived at the village and knocked on the door of the first farmhouse we saw. A woman answered and asked us what we wanted. Irene spoke only Hungarian, so I spoke for us.

In German, I said, "We are from a concentration camp. Please, do you have any food for us? We are very hungry. We haven't eaten in a week."

"No, I don't have any food," she answered and closed the door in our faces.

We tried at the next house and got the same response. It went on like this for some time. Irene wanted to quit and go back, but I did not give up.

Finally, at one house, a plump girl, my age, with long, blond hair and wearing beautiful, clean, warm clothes, opened the door. In the corner of the room, on the floor, I saw a small bowl with food in it.

"Please, a little food, a piece of bread, anything," I begged.

She shook her head no and started to close the door; quickly, I put my foot in the door.

"What about the food in the corner?" I asked. She looked at

us, surprised.

"That's the dog's food."

"May we have it?"

She smiled at us mockingly, shrugged her shoulders, and gave it to us. We took the bowl, feeling very fortunate. We ate every bit of it. It was the best meal we had during this long year, but we still felt hungry. I knocked on the door, gave her back her dish, and thanked her; we continued our search for food. It was raining, and we found ourselves farther and farther from the forest.

Then Irene turned to me and said, "Let's go back to where the others are."

"Irene," I said, "first, we wouldn't find them because we didn't keep track of how to return. Second, the war cannot go on for long. I'm not going back. Let's hide somewhere."

We decided to look for a place to stay. We asked at every farmhouse, but again, the answer was always "no."

Just as the situation seemed hopeless, one of the villagers told us we could stay in her barn in a small laundry room next to the pig sty. After walking in the constant rain for three weeks, we opened the door and saw a cement floor, a roof, a window, and a huge kettle with hot water. We went in and closed the door. I said to Irene, "Now, I'm not going to risk my life anymore. The war cannot go on for too long. We will stay here until it is over." She agreed with me.

We washed ourselves and our dresses in hot water—a luxury we had not experienced since we were taken away from our homes a year before. We smiled at each other with new hope, and we went to sleep on the floor. It was like a good hotel because there was no rain.

In the morning, a noise outside woke us up. We looked out the little window, and we saw German soldiers—their wagons, cars, and horses—running around in panic. We saw the officers tearing the Nazi insignia off their uniforms; others hastily changed from their uniforms into civilian clothes taken from the villagers for fear of being caught by the Allies.

A group of French prisoners of war was working for the Germans. One of the French prisoners in green overalls entered our room and looked surprised to see us there. Despite his broken German, we managed to communicate who we were and how hungry we felt. He left and a half hour later returned with a two-kilogram loaf of fresh, white bread and a package of margarine; he also brought us straw so that we would not have to sleep on the bare concrete floor. He told us that a German officer asked him to fix his car, and his price had been this bread and margarine.

We could not thank him enough and looked at the large loaf of bread in disbelief. We dared not eat it all as we did not know when the war would end and how long the bread would have to last us.

We felt very lucky. We had bread, margarine, a roof over our heads, straw to sleep on, hot water, and no SS troops around. We stayed inside the room, not wanting to risk our lives anymore. We were still prisoners, but now we were prisoners in hiding.

18 Avremele

The next morning, we woke up at daybreak and noticed a suspicious stillness outside. We looked out the window; the German soldiers, their cars, wagons, and horses were all gone. The villagers stayed in their homes, their window shutters and doors closed.

The sun came out, and it was a beautiful morning. We watched and waited; then I opened the door, and we walked outside.

Slowly, new sounds reached us—sounds of cars, tanks, and people approaching on the dirt road of the village. I noticed a caravan of tanks coming slowly; soldiers holding rifles and bayonets walked on both sides, protecting the tanks. When they were close enough, I realized that they were not German, but Russian tanks, and I started to shout, "Irene, the Russians are here. We are free! The war is over!" Irene and I hugged each other and cried.

I took a few tentative steps into the courtyard and found myself facing a tall, burly, Russian officer, six feet tall, no, ten feet tall, maybe a hundred feet tall in my eyes. We stared at each other for a long time, too startled to speak. My mind worked quickly. I knew Czech and a few words of Russian.

"Ya jestem Evrejka" (I am a Jew), I said.

"Evrejka? Du bist a Yid?" (You are a Jew?) He was surprised. "Du redst Yiddish?" (Do you speak Yiddish?) he asked.

I nodded yes.

"I am also a Jew," he said. "I am a captain in the Russian army."

Here is my liberator, my Messiah, a free Jew in uniform, I thought. God has answered my prayers and given me back my freedom. I was free to walk away and eat, sleep, and talk whenever and wherever I wished.

The officer looked at me—a frail, seventeen-year-old girl, five feet tall, seventy-five pounds. My hair, which the SS shaved off in Auschwitz a year ago, looked short and stubby. I wore a torn dress and a pair of mismatched men's shoes, stuffed with rags and paper to keep my feet warm, but I was clean.

"Meidele,[1] what is your name?" he asked me.

"Edith."

"Edi. . ." He could not pronounce it.

"Etu," I tried again, using my Yiddish name.

"Etele?" he asked, using the diminutive reserved for children.

"Yes, Etele," I said and a big smile spread over his face. "What is your name?" I asked him.

"My name is Avrum. . . Avremele. Tell me, Etele, how is it that you are alive? Are there other Jews who are alive too? Where is your family? Are you alone? How did you survive?" He went on and on with his questions. Finally, he let me talk.

"The SS evacuated us from our camp. We marched in the rain twenty to twenty-five miles a day, day and night, going in circles. Finally, we stopped in a forest; bombs fell around us. We had very little food, and people died from hunger and cold. Two days ago, I left the forest with my friend Irene, and we found

---

1. Little girl.

shelter here in this barn."

"Are there really Jewish people left alive in Europe? You are the first Jew I have met during this long and horrible war," he said. He came from Kiev, and we were between Dresden and Leipzig.

Irene came out of the barn. She could not talk to Avremele because she spoke only Hungarian, but she smiled. She sensed that we were talking about something positive. We were free; we were going home.

We became quiet for a while; Avremele stroked my cheek gently.

"Etele," he said softly, almost to himself, "I had a little sister your age who was killed by the Germans. You remind me of her." He put his hand in his pocket and pulled out a bar of soap. "Please, take it. I don't have anything else to give you." He looked at his watch and said, "I have to leave now."

I held the precious soap. I wondered if he knew how much I had missed this soap last night, at Auschwitz, and at Taucha. I didn't tell him that I didn't have soap for a whole year. I watched him walk away to join his troops. Suddenly, he turned around. "Etele, take care of yourself."

I waved goodbye until he disappeared into his unit, and I prayed to God to watch over Avremele.

It was the morning of May 8, 1945.

19 The Journey Home

I said goodbye to Avremele and never saw him again. Irene and I moved into the farmhouse. The remaining survivors from the forest came down into the village, where we stayed for two weeks.

Another Jewish officer came and started talking to me. I told him that I was a Jewish girl, and he cornered me in a stairway. He wanted to kiss me. I looked at him and said, "Aren't you ashamed of yourself for taking advantage of me? You are a Jewish officer. The other officer didn't bother me." He felt so ashamed that he left. The Russian soldiers had received an order not to touch the girls from concentration camps.

I remember the first night that we slept in a bed, a clean bed with covers. In the morning, I stepped out of bed, but my legs collapsed. I tried again, but my legs felt paralyzed. They had carried me for three weeks on the march. I didn't collapse once because if you did, the SS guards killed you. Now, my legs were telling me, "Give us a rest," so I crawled back into bed and stayed there for two more days.

In every German home we found an abundance of food—

smoked meats, sausages, cheeses, eggs, roasted chickens, and lots of bread. I could not understand why these German civilians did not give us something to eat when they had so much. They knew the Russians would take everything away from them anyway, yet they would not help starving, Jewish girls. The Russians ordered the German villagers to give the survivors food, clothing, and shelter.

We ate as much as we could, and Irene and I used to go to the barn every day to get milk. We shared a bucket of milk every day, and this gave us some strength.

We put on clean clothes and went out with other girls like ourselves. They came from all over into the village. We found bicycles—young girls with clean clothes and short hair, riding on bicycles, smiling. I will never forget this first picture of my freedom.

We never thought about where we would meet our families after the war if we survived, but after two weeks in this village, when we felt stronger, we began the long journey back home.

People started moving to the capital cities: Prague, Budapest, Bucharest, and other cities. Because of the chaos right after the war, no train schedules existed, and anyone could board a train without paying. Travel was very slow, and we would jump onto a moving train, sometimes with one leg still hanging out.

Often, we wanted to go in one direction, and the train went in another direction, but it didn't matter because we had enough time. We just were so happy that the war had ended.

We first stopped in Prague looking for relatives. People kept asking two questions: Where are you from? Did you know so and so? This is how we found out about family members and friends. A man came up to me, and I told him where I was from. He said, "Oh, your mother is alive," just like that.

"What?" I said in disbelief.

"Your mother is alive in Chust," he repeated.

"Why are you doing this to me?" I said angrily. "I already accepted that they killed my mother. Now, you're giving me hope, and it's not true." I felt so sure that I was right.

He went back to the place where he heard it. The next day he came back, looked me up, and said, "Listen, I talked to someone from Chust who spoke to your mother. She is waiting for you." I wanted so badly to believe it.

We continued on to Budapest where Irene met a friend, and we went our separate ways. She survived, but I never saw her again.

It took me more than two weeks to reach Chust, a trip that should have taken two days; finally, I came home to my mother.

When I left my mother in Auschwitz, she stayed behind with a cousin and sister-in-law. Mengele selected them to go to a labor camp in west Poland, but the three women stayed behind and hid in a closet. After the Germans left, the Russians liberated her in January of 1945. She always used to tell us, "I would have never lasted until the end of the war"—five more months—because she was so sick and run down already. Auschwitz was liberated in January of 1945. I was liberated on May 8, 1945.

After my mother was liberated, she made her way back home. Our house was vacant, and our neighbors had looted everything. Mother moved into her brother's empty house; he and his family did not survive. She stayed there for a few months, waiting and praying to see who from her family would come back.

When I first saw my mother, we ran to each other. We hugged and kissed and could not let go. The first night, we slept together holding each other tightly. The next day, Lilly arrived unexpectedly from Bucharest. Our joy was indescribable; we felt our lives were beginning again.

Then, I started to wait for my father and my brother; I waited and waited. I had a dream, the same dream over and over; every movement and word was the same: My father comes home. I run to him and hug and kiss him. I am very happy. Then, I'm angry at him and push him away saying, "Why didn't you let us know you are alive? I waited so long."

He says, "I had no way to let you know."

Finally, after many years, I realized that I didn't have the dream anymore. When I accepted the fact that he and my brother were not coming back, the dream stopped.

My father was forty-three years old, and my brother was eighteen.

They did not survive the Holocaust.

Epilogue

We never questioned our decision to leave Europe. Europe was soaked with Jewish blood, but where could we go? The only way out was through Germany, as the Communists controlled the rest of Eastern Europe.

Of all places, we went back to Germany to a displaced persons' (DP) camp. In Heidenheim, not far from Stuttgart, we waited for emigration papers. The United States had a quota system which involved years of waiting. Israel was still under the British Mandate, and we could not enter legally.

A few hundred people lived in this camp, and the American government and American Jewish organizations helped us with clothing, food, and money.

The DP camp in Heidenheim used to be a large police academy. In our huge room, 30 people slept on cots, and we ate together in a large dining room. Mainly young people lived in our camp because all the old people and children had been killed.

These camps helped bring us back to normal life. In the evenings, there was live music and dancing so that young people could get together. My sister, mother, and I lived in this camp for about two and half years, and during this time, I finished my high school education in a Jewish school in Germany.

When people met in those camps, they married very quickly. I knew a young man who met a girl at our camp, and three days after they met, they got married. Later, they moved to New York, and they are still together.

At another Jewish wedding, four men were holding the four posts of the Chuppah.[1] Women stood around the canopy holding candles. A candle represents a beautiful life. A young man holding one of the posts looked at a young woman holding a candle and said, "I like you."

"I like you too," she said.

"Do you want to get married?" he asked.

"Yes," she answered. They walked under the canopy and got married before they knew each other's names. People felt very lonely. Many of them had no one left after the war, so they got married to start a new family to belong to someone.

In the DP camp in Heidenheim, I met another Jewish, Russian officer named Michael. He came from Sarny, a small town in the Ukraine. At the beginning of the war, the Russians took Michael away. He was drafted into the Russian army and was fighting against the Germans throughout the war. The Nazis made the rest of his family dig their own graves and then shot them. His parents, grandparents, and five siblings perished this way.

One of Michael's sisters, who moved to Palestine before the war, survived. When Michael heard what happened to his family, he didn't want to go back to his home town—ever. People don't call Michael a survivor, but I call all European Jews survivors—whether they were in concentration camps or not—because Hitler's plan was to kill them all.

Michael wanted to get married, but I said, "I want to finish school. I'm in no rush." Unlike most other couples at the DP

---

1. A wedding canopy under which Jewish couples marry.

Camp, we dated for two years.

One day, I came home from school, and my mother said to me, "Mozel Tov [congratulations]. On Lag B'Omer[2] you are getting married."

"Why?" I said. "I'm still in school."

She explained, "I had a dream about your father, and he said, 'What is this schlepping around, a boy and a girl? Either you get married or you stop going out.'"

We were married on May 27, 1948—the same month and year that Israel became a state. I am still married to the same man today.

We left for Israel as part of the last illegal Aliyah[3] in 1948. Israel's War of Independence was going on. The military immediately drafted Michael, and he was fighting in a war once again. In 1956, he also fought in the Sinai Campaign.

We lived in Ramat Gan. My daughters, Ester and Shula, were born in Israel. I wanted to attend a teacher's institute to become a teacher. They needed teachers, but the head of the school told me that I was too old to be a student: I was 26. This was one of the big disappointments of my life, but I overcame it later.

In 1959 we moved to Los Angeles. Michael and I went back to school to complete our education, which had been interrupted by the war. In America, Michael and I attended Fairfax High School in the evenings to learn English. After two months, the teacher said that we could go to college. We took this as a big compliment. Then, I went to Santa Monica City College while in my early thirties. No one told me I was too old. The students were very polite and friendly. They may have thought I was an instructor. Then, I attended The University of Judaism and earned my teaching credential. I have been teaching children since 1965.

Michael continued his education and earned an M.A. from the University of Judaism and a Ph.D. from Hebrew Union College in Jewish history.

2. A minor Jewish holiday and popular wedding date.
3. Immigration to Israel.

We feel blessed to have our two daughters and four grand-children living near us.

Lilly lives in Israel with her family. My mother also lived in Israel until she died peacefully in her sleep at the age of 82. I was one of the very few survivors who saw my mother grow old. When we had my mother's gravestone engraved, we added the names of my father and brother: Shabtai Slomovits and Ya'akov Slomovits.

After The War

Lilly, Mother, and Edith, 1947

Monument in memory of the victims
of the Holocaust from Chust (Hust), Israel

Old police academy converted to displaced persons' camp in
Heidenheim, Germany.

Administrative officer in DP Camp in Heidenheim:
Michael Singer (1946)

Michael Singer in 1947

Edith Slomovits in 1947

Edith and Michael in 1947

Mir hobn dem kowed ajnculadn Ajch ojf unzer

CHASENE

welche wet forkumn donersztik dem 27. Mai 1948
in München, Ismaninger-Straße 48
3 a zejger nochmitog.

Edit Schlomovits   Michael Singer

Wedding invitation in Yiddish

Michael and Edith Singer's marriage on May 27, 1948

 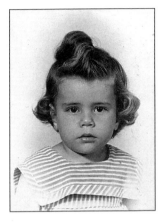

Ester Singer in 1953   Shula Singer in 1959

Boat trip to America in 1959

Graduation class of 1965, University of Judaism
(Edith Singer is third seated from right).

Dear Savta,
   You are my hero.
   I am sitting on the grass next to the womens' bunkers in Birkenau, and all I can think of is how you possibly survived this. I am here, were you were trapped when you were my age, and I'm free. Even as a free Jew I feel blackness and disgust and sorrow ~~here~~ here. I can barely stop the tears from flowing. How did you come out of this hell and manage to create the wonderful life you lead? where did you get all of this strength and courage from? After we toured the dark barracks and the "toilette" area, the group sat down and I spoke about you and your bravery. I told my friends how you risked your own life to help Lily and your mother. I told them about your tattoo and how you got it on 'ה, your birthday. Everyone came up ~~to me~~ afterwards with words of amazement, praise, and respect for you. And I thought, they don't even know the half of your bravery and unbelievable stories. I am filled with astonishment for what you withstood and SURVIVED. You continued your life and started anew, and I applaud the immense will power and strength that requires. You marched to freedom; you fought for it. I am lucky enough to get freedom without the fight, and I will not put it to waste. I will make sure that your story and the millions of perished Jews' stories are not forgetten. seeing Auschwitz has punctured my heart forever and shown me that I cannot let my own freedom go unused. ~~I can~~ Even after walking through the gas chambers I am still unable to picture the horrors of the Holocaust. But I feel pain and anger. I want to scream and cry and then learn that this never really happened. It is so overwhelming. Thank you for telling me your stories. You, a survivor, symbolize the strength and will to live that my friends and I all need as we walk through Birkenau. I love you so much.

                              Love,
                              Eve
                              חוה   auschwitz, 6/2006

Letter written by Eve Singer Arbel (Edith's granddaughter
through Shula) while visiting Auschwitz in 2006 at the age of 16,
the same age that Edith was during her imprisonment.

Acknowledgements

With special thanks to my husband and best friend, Michael, who encouraged me to write.

To my daughter, Shula, who spent countless hours editing and typing my stories.

To my daughter, Ester, who coordinated the publishing of this book.

And to Jim Zuckerman, who gave of his time and photographic talents.